# Dandelion Dreams
# and Other Poems

# Dandelion Dreams and Other Poems

Edward J. Steinhardt

DORMER WINDOW BOOKS

Published by Dormer Window Books
Post Office Box 771795
St. Louis, MO 63177

Library of Congress Cataloging in Publication Data

Steinhardt, Edward, J., 1961-
    Dandelion Dreams and Other Poems.
    I. Title
99-96226, 1999  811'54
ISBN: 0-9641235-1-7

Manufactured in the United States of America
First printing, December, 1999
10 9 8 7 6 5 4 3 2 1

Acknowledgments:

"The Ringleader" first appeared in *Among the Trees,* a joint anthology between the Columbia Chapter of the Missouri Writers' Guild and The Ink Club.

"Imaginary Gardens with Real Toads in Them" was first read during a ceremony honoring Marianne Moore, at Grace Episcopal Church, Jefferson City, Missouri, November 18, 1989.

"Attending the Memorial," in honor of Howard Nemerov, was read April 26, 1992 during the closing ceremony of Missouri Writers Week, featuring Richard Wilbur, in Hermann, Missouri.

"The Shadowlands" was first read during the 80th anniversary ceremony for the Missouri Writers' Guild, April 23, 1995, in the Rotunda of the Missouri State Capitol, Jefferson City.

"Queen of Hearts" first appeared in the *Montgomery County Standard.*

*Thy winged seeds, whereof the winds take care,*
*Are like the words of poet and sage*
    *Which through the free heaven fare,*
*And, now unheeded, in another age*
*Take root, and to the gladdened future bear*
*That witness which the present would not heed,*
    *Bringing forth many a thought and deed,*
*And, planted safely in the eternal sky,*
*Bloom into stars which earth is guided by.*

—from "To the Dandelion"
by James Russell Lowell

*for Peggy Nemerov*

R·E·L·A·T·I·O·N

# N·A·T·U·R·E

# S·P·I·R·I·T

S·O·L·O

# Introduction

ONCE LONG AGO I naively asked Ezra Pound his opinion of James Joyce. EP drew back quizzically and answered, "Do you mean the man or the work?" From my question, in which I meant to refer to Joyce's early poems, and EP's reply I at once realized that, although the poet and the poem are discrete, they are also a unique synthesis in which only the poet's voice may long outlive the poet.

This introduction is only a brief and inadequate appreciation of Edward J. Steinhardt, the man and the work. In his earlier book, *The Painting Birds*, Steinhardt already displayed the broad vision of experienced poets and artists. Its more than a hundred poems— tender, tough, ironic, reverent, personal and impersonal— are acutely observant lyrical commentaries unbridled by time, topic or geography. The droll poems remind us of our sublimity; the sublime make us recognize our mutability.

Now in this expansive collection of *Dandelion Dreams* Steinhardt brings us (as Lowell described) both the promise and permanence of the poet's voice. Dream and reality both seem distinct from each other. Yet how can we separate them except as concept and action? "If poetry is a dream" William Hazlitt wrote, "the business of life is much the same. If it is a fiction, made up of what we wish things to be, and fancy that they are, because we wish them so, there is no other nor better reality." William Butler Yeats put it more succinctly: "In dreams begins responsibility," a phrase quoted from an old play.

As a Romantic, Hazlitt defined poetry as "the language of the imagination and the passions." Although many of today's poets repudiate imagination and wince at the word "passions," both terms still apply to the most powerful poems of our time.

Poetry has long endured many definitions (and indeed I've noted that each poet formulates his/her own definition of poetry); but all definitions of poetry are based on its process: how it is created through knowledge and experience, observation and intuition, all of which nurture the imagination and (Wordsworth's favorite term) emotions. The process evolves into language, form and style, the elements used in rudimentary analysis of poetry.

In free verse form, with few exceptions (e.g., "Indian Spring, Indian Summer: The Cave"), Edward Steinhardt observes life. His poems are revealing but not "confessional." Life experiences enter his lines, often subtly, for a larger purpose. His ability to imagine and celebrate that life, not only in maturity but also in childhood, are exceptional. Childhood, for instance, is expressed exquisitely in poems like "Pieno di Rammarchi," "Lost and Found" and in passages of longer poems like "The Shadowlands."

Another remarkable poem is "Hide and Seek," in which more is implied ("A symbiotic balance between/ The hunter and the hunted") than a simple children's game. There are also deep contrasts: the warmth of love, as in the "Jennifer" poems, and the immobile, frozen landscapes in "Snowspell" and other poems on snow themes.

There are haunting narratives like "Gone-away Lake," "The Missouri River at Dusk" and "Night Demons." Rustic imagery of work and play ("Mowing," "Two Boys in a Field") skillfully shifts to urban settings in Missouri and elsewhere. From the warm opening tableau of July Fourth to the closing poem, "Remembering the Dreams" this collection is replete with honest and authentic American life in the finest traditions of such greatly neglected poets as Edgar Lee Masters, E.A. Robinson, Maxwell Bodenheim and others early in our century.

Finally, Edward J. Steinhardt is a poet of abiding loyalties— to family, to friends (including especially his late friend Howard Nemerov) and to the principles of journalistic integrity which we find, subtly or openly, affecting his poetry. For Steinhardt, the man is the dream and the work reality. His book *Dandelion Dreams* is the work of one touched by many ages and cultures— but it is an American original.

—Charles Guenther

R·E·L·A·T·I·O·N

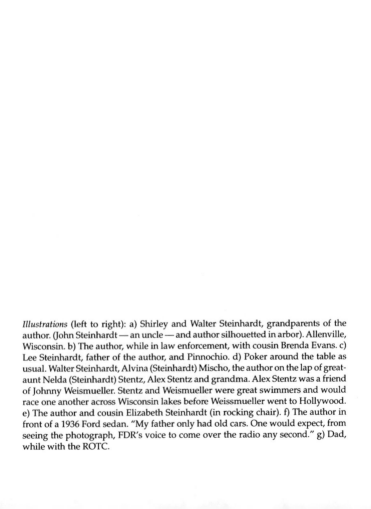

*Illustrations* (left to right): a) Shirley and Walter Steinhardt, grandparents of the author. (John Steinhardt — an uncle — and author silhouetted in arbor). Allenville, Wisconsin. b) The author, while in law enforcement, with cousin Brenda Evans. c) Lee Steinhardt, father of the author, and Pinnochio. d) Poker around the table as usual. Walter Steinhardt, Alvina (Steinhardt) Mischo, the author on the lap of great-aunt Nelda (Steinhardt) Stentz, Alex Stentz and grandma. Alex Stentz was a friend of Johnny Weismueller. Stentz and Weismueller were great swimmers and would race one another across Wisconsin lakes before Weissmueller went to Hollywood. e) The author and cousin Elizabeth Steinhardt (in rocking chair). f) The author in front of a 1936 Ford sedan. "My father only had old cars. One would expect, from seeing the photograph, FDR's voice to come over the radio any second." g) Dad, while with the ROTC.

# On Holiday, July Fourth

*for Pat Hudson*

You sat in the shade of a forsythia bush
And cut the ends off green beans
While I painted your summer kitchen,
Even though it now only houses
A deep freeze, entry, and indoor john.

It didn't bother me at all
That you sat there in the shade
While I climbed ladders
Putting primer on your house.
Our conversation there in the July humidity
Only magnified what
Our friendship has come to be:
You, married; me, the single,
Weekend hired man,
Exchanging past and present reminiscences
And decent gossip.

Even when Dick sweated around the corner
And you chastised him for using
A wet receptacle for collecting beans,
I could see the nibbling love
That the two of you share,
And your kind gracious meals at noontime
Reminiscent of my Grandma,
Whose hands only fixed me food I liked.

It was a total splendor in the country,

I say, including when 12 year-old Mark
From across the road
Joined us for bagels.  That was good, too:
Three generations talking things
We'll never remember—
Except Mark's proud display
Of his hat signed by Ozzie Smith.

All in all, it was a pretty neat Fourth.
Even when the sun took your shade
You stuck it out, and stayed there
To chat that extra while.
That's when friendship serves
As a panacea: stroking the house,
Minding the cats,
Painting the roses,
Chasing the shadows that bring relief.

# Traveling Through Jasper County, Missouri

I am struck twice by the sight
Of burning leaves aside a service road
Farmhouse: the remembrance
Of burning leaves in youth,
And the fall regularity
Of that mystic toxic aroma that bade
Good memories of boyhood:
A romping dog, a boy— not to mention
A safe pre-pubertal arson.

I pass a blue Chevy listing badly
To one side due to some heavy women.
So these are the flatlands,
Raised to an elevation to send me down
Manageable hills toward Oklahoma.
The barns and decapitated silos
Stand sentinel to those going west.
A sign goes past announcing the home
Of George Washington Carver;
Not even a swoosh, or a sigh.
It just goes past, a mute verbage made alive
Only with someone else's mental magic.
*Tulsa. 116 miles.*
That sign goes by, too.
The sun has begun to climb down into my eyes.
I squint. A car from Texas
Passes me in the direction I am going;
Another universe of lives at a warp speed
Of 75 miles per hour speeding west.
They are soon lost, eclipsed by a slow rise of road.

*Turkey Creek.* I neither saw it
Nor could peer back without losing my grip
On the road. There still must be turkeys here,
Strutting out of sight in the scattered wood.
Wait— a Sunday construction work,
The road is numerous with those concrete barriers.
The eye of the needle, I call it.

I am entering Springfield.
Maybe not. *44-West Tulsa* assures me
That my heading is right.
The roads going east and west are closer now.
The silhouettes of souls go by unmarked
And unidentified, faceless shapes speeding east.
I can see into cars I pass,
Looking at the backs of heads.
Yes, now I'm alongside;
No, I must look forward.
We must not connect our metal.
I see only part of a face.
What are the sights, smells
And sounds in that car?
It is a new car. I remember
The aroma of a new car's interior.

*Last exit before Oklahoma. Toll Road.*
I saw that sign. Logic and maturity replace
    surprise.
Must I pay? No, that was an exit.
*Entering Will Rogers Turnpike. Toll Road.*
Oh my. I'm in Oklahoma and I must pay.
*$2.50 for 42 miles.* That's six cents a mile.

I shall fall in behind this 18-wheeler
And go this space on his draft, his wake;
And at a good 75. I hope Oklahoma cops
Do not disguise their cars in Mustangs.
I go forward.

# Thanksgiving

*for Elizabeth Stevens*

It is the night
Before Thanksgiving.
Men and wives
Whisper among themselves
From their beds,
Exchanging marital gossip
(As man and wife
Share everything—
Ask a deacon's wife)
About the relatives
Who have come to possess
The living room divan,
The fold-out couch—
And, in the case of kids—
Sleeping bags.

This November holiday
Has imparted visions
To everyone of like blood,
A mass gravitation
Toward the nearest
(Or farthest) dearest
Relative this Thanksgiving.
Carloads coast
Into destination
To lay claim
To the guest rooms
And whisper whispers

Everyone cranes to hear,
Like: "How tall Timmy is,"
"Did you see what that kid
Gets away with?" or
"What time should
We leave tomorrow?"

Thanksgiving in its way
Brings the family home.
With school out,
Loved ones embrace,
Kiss, smile,
(Or just hold back)
In this short holiday
Of cranberries, turkey,
And apple pie.

Great care is taken even
Not to disagree;
To always say the best things,
And make the day pass
With Macy's, the NFL,
And the precursory
"How have you been,"
Without getting much
Better than that
During commercials.

The children frolic,
Or have absolutely
Nothing to do
With the remaindered

Or cast-off cousins,
Who trust in their
Own universes
Before any family reunion.

The tenure of family
Is contingent
On a recipe of love,
Phone, distance,
Familiarity, and
"We've got to get together
Again real soon."
Love is prorated
By holiday
And the anticipation
Of having relatives over,
Until familiarity
Breeds contempt past
The first smiles of hello
And the revolving
Pantry door
That speaks louder
Than the best mother
One may adore.

Once the turkey
Has been reduced
To sandwiches, and
Then to skeletal form,
It's time to move
The family on,
Throw water on the fire,

And take the wagon home.
Thanksgiving, sometimes,
Is an American pilgrim's
License to gorge,
Get fat, and be justified
By a legal holiday.

## Hide and Seek

The children who play the game
Gather at dusk near the biggest house;
The largest yard,
And bring their number together
For the count.

This game, this game of hide and seek,
Is the primal instinct of the hunt;
For in losing one's self in the shadows,
Under the porch, or high on a limb,
The boy or girl commits his length
To camouflage, winning by being
Out of sight, eluding the predator
Who must count to an agreed-on
Number, civilizing, trivializing
A looked-for past-time,
A symbiotic balance between
The hunter and the hunted.

The boy or girl who must get
His numbers right, seldom does.
The contract calls for one hundred,
But single digits are skipped for ten.
The comrades who know
The contract is a lie
Run nervously helter-skelter
For the *best* hide-a-way—
The one already claimed
By the voice that impatiently pleads:
"*Not* here," a squatter's forethought:

The strawberry of a seemingly
Original mutually-shared inspiration.

The child who pretends to hide
Behind his hands, a tree,
Or the corner of the house,
Completes his digits
And stalks quickly his brother,
Or neighbor, listening for the rustles,
The unintended footfall;
The whispers that fix
The course of destination—
Surprise and unveiling...

The game of hide and seek
Is an infrequent summer sport,
A fast lesson in the time
It takes to seek and find
Those who are more and less clever:
To retrace another's steps
By plan or happenchance;
That in coming out of darkness,
The children trade places
Of the hunter and the hunted.
In the brilliance of the human mind,
The game remains a game—
At least until the parents call
And say it is time to come in
From one night's half-hour
Of anxious terrestrial flight.

## The Evening Eaves

It's midnight.  And the wind
Is howling around the corners
Of the house.
And it's keeping me awake.

                    And thinking.

Where are we as a people, each one?
Here I lie in lower-class opulence:
A baseboard heater, a quilt,
And a lamp in the shape
Of a cherub lighting this page.

The wind blows from west to east.
Who else does it seek in its path?
The homeless man in St. Louis
Sleeping in old junkyard cars?
The teenager hitching rides on I-70
With the next 18-wheeler
That rolls into Rosey's Cafe?

Or maybe it's the young couple
With their electric just cut off...
And the one-gallon plastic milk jugs
Filled with water over in the corner—
With just a little frost on the lids...

Or maybe it's the old woman—
In or out of her mind—
Opening a can of cat food

Because it's a quarter cheaper
Than real tuna.

Or maybe it's Sparky
Who cleans up at the local bar.
The bartender lets him fry up
The surplus shrimp after he's
Cleaned up for the night—
And doesn't pull off the tails.

Or maybe it's the kid
Two streets over who ate
Surplus cheese for dinner tonight—
And for dessert was treated
To a peanut butter sandwich.
Bread's getting so expensive these days...

And here I am wondering,
Wondering at the commonality of it all,
The injustice, the different crosses
Each person singularly bears.
One couple goes to bed
With a million bucks in the bank,
And any given family
Goes to bed with nary a thing
To show in the cupboard.

One man dreams of grandiose plans:
The stock exchange, CDs, and IRAs;
Another man dreams of how
He can one day take his family
Out from government welfare

And the Chickory Street housing projects.
Another man, two weeks into the same
Cardboard box in an alley somewhere
Just dreams of an ample well-done
Seven-ounce ribeye steak...

The wind is still blowing.
It's twenty-three days into the new year.
And it's cold outside.
The thawing of day has been replaced
By little frozen streams
That halt in the street.
The wind and lunar light offer up
A lonely, desolate moonscape—
This winter of many discontents.

The storm windows rattle as if on cue.
We've now entered the long sleep,
Trading daydreams for those of the night;
Dreaming to escape, escaping to dream;
The wind howling in our ears,
"Aunty Em', Aunty Em'."
And all the houses fall—
                              Asleep.

## Dog Days

This month Iraq "annexed" Kuwait
As its southernmost province.
Isn't that quaint.

The invasion took us all by surprise,
I'm afraid.  I remember when the Iraqis
Massed on the Kuwaiti border.
I *remember* that.

I went downtown in our little town
To mail some bills
In the outside drop at the post office.
The town tonight, being Friday,
Is unusually active, with dozens
Of big souped-up pickups
Parked in local parking lots.
Men, three to a cab,
Yak, pass beer, blare horns
And offer pronounced daring stares
As you approach:
"Yeah, What are you gonna do about it?"

Four men sit in the back
Of a big idling Ford.  One sits
In the corner by the tailgate
Nonchalantly holding a Busch beer
Atop the side-panel.
Some men are quiet, some are rancorous;
Most with nothing to do.
The police do nothing.

As I go home, I search myself
For understanding
As my anger boils upward
And my hands grip the wheel
The short distance home.
I resent these men who are idle,
Who have homes, some who have children —
And nothing to do.
In the greater spectrum of life
We must surely put
More back into society
Than obscenities and empty, rancid
Beer cans the businessman
Must pick up in the morning.

Part of this dispute with Iraq
Invading Kuwait is over oil.
I resent idle men who idle big trucks
With big gas tanks.
Each of us has a universe.
And how we cause our stars to shine
And planets to turn
Must be for the common good.

This evening my brother
Is in the boiler room
Of a destroyer in the Persian Gulf.
I say we need a few good men.
Hang in there, Wally.

## Merry Christmas, Delmar

There is a war being waged on Delmar.
A wrong turn in December
And I see row upon row of old houses;
Once beautiful townhouses— many of them.
The People's Clinic sports a banner,
"We have always cared."
The clinic is boarded up.
An old service station is burned-out.
Yards are accumulated dumping grounds.
Every fourth house is windowless,
"No Trespassing By Order Of
The City Of St. Louis," the signs say.

It is 35 degrees with a threat
Of snow in the air.
There are only a few people out.
One or two walk in the street
Where the sidewalks are gone.
Where have the people gone?
To the turreted rooms here
That know only space heaters,
Stray cats, gunshots and graffiti?
Here among the rubble
Of Victorian dreams?
An old Cadillac has a giant
Red ribbon on its radiator.

I take Delmar as far as it goes.
I come out at Powell Hall.
The Fox Theatre is playing

*A Christmas Carol.*
On Grand, I stop at a light.
An old prostitute
With flaming red hair crosses.
She wears a big coat down to her knees.
Silk slacks, the pattern
Of dark green Victorian wallpaper
Ripple in the wind.
I try to see her eyes.
She could be anyone's mother—
Anyone's aunt.
A young black man on the corner
With his hands in his pockets
Watches me watch her.
The whites of his dark eyes
Dart from me to her;
From her to me.
The light changes.
Kenny G is playing
Christmas music on the radio.
I shudder, and clutch the truck home.
Merry Christmas, Delmar.

# Cousins

*for Elizabeth*

We are cousins of the earth
Molded from close seed.
Separated as toddlers we have neither
The Lincoln Logs nor proximity.
Two months apart
We are kin only by blood,
Separated by a mental window
That fogs only on one side.
I am daily reminded
Of our two buoyant faces
Frozen in an old Polaroid
I keep in the hall.

Now, for distance and memory's part,
You are gone.
Electrical impulses keep
The waving pictures
In a brainbox flailing for the past.
It is no comfort fitting into the space
Between our black and white faces
In a simple rocking chair
And a scared, present,
Apprehensive curiosity.
You're only a phone call away.
And I don't.

Now, I wouldn't know you if I saw you.
Grandma used to have a tilting frame

Showing a beautiful, bronzen face.
Now you make babies
And have given up our name.
I sit in a dim room
In an overstuffed chair
And write how things used to be.

# P

The art of apology, I suppose,
Is spanking pride
And kneeling standing up.
And since you said your words,
And I mine, it probably
Makes us pretty Even Steven.

We're never really fully born
Until we die— and the difference
Between breath and exit
Is the Manufacturer's guarantee
That we are now after Milton's Paradise
Less-bent for evil and more divine.
The best insurance for that, simply,
Is a tattle-tale heart.

You may remember
That last lunar eclipse
When the earth's shadow
Moved swiftly past
Our one orbiting moon;
Then the ephemeral crimson
That lingered and was gone
When the moon was returned
Its natural lunar light.

Eclipses are rare.
By the healing hand of nature
(And God's respite)
We are given back a second chance—
And the steady assurance

Of our one dark evening's
Surrogate sun.

# Paper Pictures

*In memory of all the innocent
who have died in Bosnia*

The great lines that stood
To see the show
Snaked through the halls
With children in tow.

Now this one, said the guide,
Is one of our treasured pieces:
Three leaves flat on water
Beneath a Bosnian slaughter.

We stand enraptured
Looking betwixt the leaves
To see the knives
Held to children on knees.

We do the doubletake,
Having discovered the camera's eye
That panned the butcher
Of the innocent who died.

Upon leaving, I remembered
An NPR special on Bosnia
When a daughter and mother
Cried for the sister's brother,

Who had been taken captive
On the homeplace there

By a unit of soldiers
Who laughed with eyes that glared.

Must I go? the young man asked.
I play basketball, he said.
You'll play basketball again;
They patted his head.

The teenager was taken to a barn.
And careful to keep their distance,
The mother and sister followed behind
To see what they could find.

The soldiers took the young man
And forced him to his knees.
They drew a knife across his neck
Like an animal left to bleed.

His mother and sister came
And cradled this brother and son,
The woman and daughter wailed
As to why this deed was done.

In the telling of the story,
The family wept on the radio—
And I, a listener, listened
As I never listened before.

I sobbed for them, us all,
The humanity: a boy,
Slain there on the floor.

# Billiards

*for Brian Horstmann*

The game takes up
Considerable room—
Laid on its back on four legs,
With six holes
That nab your balls
Sooner than you can spit
And send 'em
Through a network of tunnels
The Pyramid of Giza would envy.
And when done, the balls roll
To a compact stop
In solid or striped arrangement,
Down near where
You put your quarter in.

I like pool.
Mark Twain liked pool.
Where else can you take a stick,
Call out your pocket
And send a shiny black ball
In the direction of your opponent?
It's good.  It's fair.
Where else can two
Come to the table,
Peer through florescent
Light and smoke,
Wave sticks at one another,
And chalk another one up?

## A Visit Home

It was the first visit home—
In two months.  How things change.
There are bluebird houses up now
At Mom and Dad's
And a lean-to against the garage
(The last building he's going
To build, says Dad)
And a thousand frogs
Chorusing the month of May.

As we stood there in the porch light,
Out of the circle of attacking bugs
But well within the tentative
Circle of goodbye
That some families engage in
Who do not touch one another,
I asked, "Where's Caesar?"
(The ten-year-old Cocker Spaniel
Poodle who was *always* around).
"Oh," Dad said.  "He's gone.
We think the sons-a-bitches shot him,"
Making reference to the neighbors
Who more than once
Had bitches in heat.
"We looked along the road—
But we didn't find 'im."

I am saddened, and also marvel
At Caesar's long stay among us—
From whining pup to pudgy dog

Whose only redeeming feature—
It seemed—
Was that you didn't know
If he was looking at you
When you scolded him
Because of the curls of hair
That screened his eyes.

"How long has he been gone?" I asked.
"About two months," said Father.
That's just how long it's been
Since I've been back.
Tonight, it will be a long time
Getting home.
It will be even longer
Coming back.

# To a Fellow in Correspondence

I
NEW YEARS

You spoke, dear fictitious Byron,
Of a shroud— that save
A covering of snow that covers earth,
Was nothing else but Christ Himself.
Indeed!

You write dismally and poetically
To a dismal fellow who neither understands
The regularity or fallacy
Of the present season, but finds
A steady cheer in the fact
That the sun does not rise
For months on end in the polar regions.
And thinking that, I am duly comforted
As one who is only partly raped
By the present season.

New Year's came in the size
Of a football— for those who watch
The stuff, so I neither enjoyed the tube
Nor much else for that matter.
The only calming solace
Was that all the banks were closed
And my money was not spent any faster.

I know not what the new year
Will bring, but I shall get along.

And you will, too.
I, on all accounts, am only
A "feeble-minded commoner" as you say.
And I like that.
But in this timely dreary season
I look again for the splendid
Rites of spring.

## Daylight Savings Time

Thanks for calling tonight, friend.
It was nice chatting about the old days
When we both were young.
But tonight I feel youth
Is a departed son, a box of cherished
Children's toys shut up in an attic
Somewhere— that has meaning to only
One blond, bare-headed kid
Who got sunburns, played solitary games,
And squeamishly lifted a slimy frog
To be frozen in a black-and-white
Photograph.

Youth is a paradise lost,
When innocence— or ignorance—
Is the byword of a free-wheeling spirit:
Exploring, experimenting,
Testing the life of things.

A little dog was part of that.
Small puppy Lucky was a sense of youth,
When boy was companion to the dog
Until one day the canine demonstrated
Rabies in a strawberry patch
And had to be put out of his misery.
And Lucky was buried in the corner
By the fence.
Wishing wouldn't bring him back,
Though there was a small boy's
Temptation to dig him up

30

And bring him back.

All the wishing in the world
Cannot bring those years back again.
And thank God for wishing.
We would be nothing without it—
Only extant animals on a clump of rock
Orbiting a fiery star
Surviving only to survive
With no aspirations higher than our heads.
We're much better than that.

Tonight, Daylight Savings
Takes away an hour
To be given back in the fall.
Some things we have little to say about.
Such is life.
Youth is taken away to be credited
To some old man in a nursing home somewhere;
Who finds a small comfort
In dreaming dreams
Of one small boy and one small dog
Running with the dragonflies.

## The Magazines

Sit there in the convenience store
Just within temptation
In the peripheral view
That makes you pause, start,
And stride away.
You take great pains
To see who's looking.

There is some promise
In this parade of human flesh.
We know by looking
That the average man or woman
Does not look like this,
Nor jumps into leather (or lather)
To a cameraman's cue.

We, ourselves, hold our appendages
In some fashion of regard.
The faces that peer from slick covers
Smile— but cry in the eyes.
We are all voyeurs in some way,
Looking in, looking out.
We have mutually
Gotten what we came for,
Paid for it, and taken the change.

We hit the door.
No refunds, no returns.

## The Gasconade Boatyards

It sometimes comes back,
You know, the visions
Of what dead eyes no longer see.
If you look right over there,
You'll see the gaunt buildings
That comprise a local history
That brought World War II
Closer to home than you would know:
The Gasconade Boatyards.

It's hard to believe these days
A couple dozen German
Prisoners-of-war labored there,
Where the two rivers—
Missouri and Gasconade— merge.
But they did. These fathers,
Brothers, husbands, worked
Their tenure for being caught
On the wrong side of history
To build the boats the U.S. Army
Corps had them build right there.

The Germans were treated well,
Made friends among
Their American counterparts,
And eventually found their way
Home at the close of the war:
To their fathers, brothers,
Sisters, wives, and mothers.
In war, you do your time,

Run scared, pray on the mercy
Of your captor, and get in line.
The Germans here, at any rate,
Fared better than most in a war
That was not generally sympathetic
To the enemy.

I am told that when the Germans
Were trucked through Hermann
They stopped and pissed
Where the VFW stands now.
This I am told by an old gent
I do not remember—
Who remembers that war I talk about.
I write this for him,
With the best intent
That this roughshod history may infer.
May we always know what happened there
At the Gasconade Boatyards,
And the soldiers of either side
Who gestured, prayed, and labored there.

## To a Former Bachelor

Driven by nativity, lust,
And the double bed,
You have chosen to forsake
The precursory order of single,
Free, and lowly men
Who have chosen by design
(Or out of range of Cupid's darts)
To withstand the mysteries
Of the marriage bed,
The married tax return,
Joint checking and baby crib,
Toward which most men
Are drawn by curiosity—
If not to live more cheaply,
You said.

# The Forest Through the Trees

*for Wade Frye*

I do not know what advice
I may give to you, Wade,
Being half my age
And knowing more
Than when I was there
Where you are now;
You, who has a sprinting 16 years
On your side—
And many more to go.

Simply, I suppose,
Let no one look down
On your youth, Wade:
Though balance your universe
With respect, honor—  even God.
These three, diligently earned—
Easily lost—
Are treasures unheard of these days
In the age of "me" and "me."

There are some who would
Have you forsake your own
Special identity,
And take the shorter route,
The faster run,
And do the carnival round;
While a larger sphere
Spins, reflects and holds us here—

So deeply in receding wood
Bound on all sides by blue.

Keep your face straight
And your eyes turned
Toward whatever prize
You may come to hold in your heart.
Then, should trouble and sorrow
Come (and it will),
You will be ready,
Ready as you will be
Seeing through trees
Dead in winter
While snow blows your way
Stiff against the face,
Bringing tears out
Of unwanted necessity:
Crying for the pain—
Keeping the will—
Seeing the forest through the trees.

# Reruns

A guy on NPR said today
That quite a few
Television shows these days
Are old serials
We used to watch.
"It's like the seventies
All over again," I believe
He said.

Some things are cyclical.
The Chaldeans were,
Stonehenge is,
Those crop circles in England are;
God knows crop rotation is,
Sometimes societal morals—
Even *morels* in season...
We're as cyclical
As the weather cycles
The weatherman talks about.
Heck, we're born to die.

I wouldn't mind seeing
The CBS Sunday Evening Mysteries
Again myself.
I've got to see Columbo
Put that smoking hand
To his forehead and say,
"Excuse me, I almost forgot..."

# Pitching Things

*for Mike Heying*

I save everything.
People twice or three times my age
Are accused of a solitary insanity
When they die, when the relatives
Come to pitch things out.

When I was in school,
A friend and I
Snuck into a people-less house
Two eccentric sisters
Left to fill another.
We climbed in a window
At dusk and walked close paths
Among wardrobes
(with clothes still in them);
Furniture, a kitchen,
And living room
Complete and ready
For the family ghosts
To come clanging home
And pick up where they left off.

As uninvited guests,
We purveyed what was forbidden:
A house locked in time
There among the trees
Along the street— a material
Temptation to two teenage boys

Whose summer idleness
Included a good-natured
Breaking and entering.

What I remember most
About the house was the one,
Single upstairs room— a bedroom—
Sequestered up above.
I marveled at the old oil lamp
That hung on a wall,
The turn-of-the-century kind
With the round convex
Mirror behind.
I was struck by the plainness
And practicality of a lamp
Fingers once turned down;
A hand that reached up
Toward the flame,
Turning the wick onto itself:
Its fire reflective, dancing,
Bowing to a single audience—
Then darkness.

It was an odd illumination
Atop a good flight of stairs—
For one or two women.
There was electric downstairs,
To be sure.  The old lines
Traveled side by side
From insulator to insulator:
Twins with the same genetic code.

We left the house, my friend and I,
Having seen its secrets we never
Dared talk about after that.
We stepped silently
Through stacks of magazines
And piles of raccoon dung,
Exclaiming just loud enough
To cringe on cue, but low enough
For the neighbors not to hear.
We stepped quickly and vaulted
Our young men's window
From past to present,
Landing in the underbrush.
We strolled the rooms as curators,
But dared touch nothing.

# A Protest Poem

X.

# At Union Station, St. Louis

The trains don't pull
Through Union Station anymore.
Now it's full of shops,
A hotel— a country boy's
Version of the Sistine Chapel.
Only the American-version kiosks
Wheel along the tile floor.

When you get off the train now,
You're under an overpass.
It looks like Lawrence, Kansas
After the bomb. . .
You carry your luggage
Up to or through a trailer house,
Pre-fab station.
Station masters look like
Off-duty police officers.

Newcomers, without a car,
Stumble among the potholes.
Union Station rises in the distance,
Looking like the Emerald City
On Pay-per-View.
They may not let you in.
The towers rise above the street
Where statues, disanimated,
Frolic between the avenues.

You carry your own bags.
The wizard will come out,

Perchance, with a team of horses—
Maybe even some midgets.
Hopefulness is one step less
Than helplessness.  Cars drive past
With the windows rolled up,
The doors locked.

Welcome to Oz.
Welcome to the Emerald City.
Thank you for using Amtrak.
The Flexliner was here last month.
Too bad you missed it.
You missed a lot of things.
Two homeless guys
Watched a tourist get mugged
Last week.  Walk fast.
Wear sensible shoes.
Get inside the station,
The City of Refuge.
A Blues band played in the station
Yesterday among the shoppers.
Yes, Blues— with a harmonica.

The lights go down,
Crime goes up.
Get to your room.
Watch the milling faces
From your balcony.
Milling faces in the act
Of getting milled.
Now that's a positive thought.
There are even bellhops.

They know where to park
Without getting a ticket.
But that doesn't help you.
You don't have a car.

Tomorrow you can see the Wizard,
The Arch— even one
Of Dred Scott's favorite places.
Take the kids, even.
Don't forget your west-bound
Tomorrow (or was it east-bound)
Go east (for me).
Maybe someone will take you
To the station tomorrow.
If not, have the kids
Count the chuckholes
On the way back— like sheep.
"Like sheep we have gone astray."
Dear me.   What have we done?
*"A-l-l Aboard!"*  The conductor
Is *really* nice this time.
He's careful to call out the stops.
Pull out the stops.
What a journey.  Do you have
What you came for now?
The man behind the curtain
Said you have, back there
With all the bells and whistles.
"We're not in Kansas anymore,  Toto."
God, that's a fact.  God.  Yeah.
The little man with the balloon.
He made it up all inside his head.

Dorothy's shoes were auctioned off
For a lot of money.
"Thank you for riding Amtrak."
Call 1-800-USA-RAIL.
It was a nice visit.
Please give my regards
To Aunty Em'. Oh, you're going east . . .
Give my regards to Broadway.
Or something like that.

# Court

The boys up the hill
The next street over
Are dribbling their basketballs
This temperate-winter evening.
The voices carry forth,
Unintelligible, but youthful
And certain.  The spot-lit drive
Sends shadows against
And away from one another,
Raising and praising the ball,
Blocking the partner
Of the other side.
In between, the suspension
Of sound in darkness
Is soon followed
By the vibration of the hoop,
And the exclamations that come
Of missing the basket—
Versus the pride of silence—
That comes when aim and throw
Come to fruition.

As in times past,
Parents, by ten o'clock,
Will come to the door
And summon the children in
From the cool, quick air
That will later draw a frost
And fog over the town by morning.
There will no longer

Be the symbiotic balance
Of youthful energy,
And the regular anticipated
Exhilaration of heart and ball
Against the darkness
That traps the breath
Of all irascible
And irreplaceable youth
Before being called in.

By custom and necessity
The boys will sleep nightly,
And dream dreams
That may or may not
Involve the game at hand:
Where aim and sportsmanship
Is true throughout the game—
Where running down the court,
You aim, shoot,
Run back to the other side,
And only hear the swishing
Of the net in your ears
To a spattering of applause
As you ready to run
Down the court again,
And again.

## Jennifer II2895

You are indeed an expressive soul.
I didn't know I'd be getting
A poet in the bargain.

It's crazy, isn't it,
Going to work and acting
Like there's nothing between us?
What a charade!  But the laugh
Will be on our friends at work
Who may have an inkling—
But not the pen; a page,
But not the book.  What a thing!

As I write this, I am passing
Highway 100 at 3:25.
I could call,
But then I would wake everyone...
Such a built-in curse!
To travel past the road to your arms
Again and again.

We shall have to talk,
I suppose, via the telephone.
We shall have to plan again
A rendezvous for at least a kiss.
All of this is a test of our love,
I am sure.
Otherwise, we would go wild
With passion, fall into a ditch,
And get run over by the ambulance.

## Jennifer III495

I feel like we are two people
Who've bought each other
On the lay-away plan;
That we cannot be complete
Until the final payment
Is made.

But the *anxiousness* is good.
The anxiousness keeps us fresh,
On our toes, bright— and
With a spark.  I never want
The spark to go.  And I don't
Think it *ever*  shall.
We ignite one another;
We inflame one another;
We are both on
A child's merry-go-round
In the park of our choosing.
We push ourselves,
Jump on, and careen
Wildly with the pleasure—
Which is what I have
When you kiss me
And hold me...

I *can't* wait 'til summer,
When we can go off together alone
And take day trips in love;
When we can share each other
In longer times: in the car,

On the street, on sidewalks of towns
We've never been.  We can take
These routes together,
Holding hands, kissing in dark corners
Of towns that do not know us;
That our familiarity will be
With each other; that in the surety
Of those times, we may become
One in mind, also— and even talk
More of God— that by all these things
We will be honored when our time
Together comes.

I want it to be a summer
Of holdings hands, shared love,
Shared knowledge, a shared Creator—
Who will endow us finally with
The peace we have just now had
A taste of; of calm, the rounding
Of the edges of our souls;
Completeness...

To these things I think daily
Beyond the perimeter of your kiss;
When I cannot touch you,
And can only call you from afar.

# Jennifer III1195

Do you know that I love you
More each and every day?
Your mind, your soul;
Your each and every way?

Do you know that I treasure
The workings of your mind;
Your creativity, your proclivity,
The hidden depths I find?

Do you know I am anxious
For the new revelation;
Of attributes and things
That will help our congregation?

Do you know that I love you
As we become one-minded;
That as time will progress
We needn't be reminded—

And that I love you all the more.

## Jennifer III1595

Well, gosh,
What can I say?

The events of Monday
Play inside my head

Awash,
Serenely jumbled;

Names mumbled,
The glance of flesh,

Intimacies,
Stopping short

Of the human fort;
Scaling the citadel,

Seeing the Pleides,
Called back,

Changing tack,
A small boy's cries,

Silence denied,
Immortally-tied,

Gosh.

## Jennifer XII395
## Remembering You

You are gone.
I read through all the poems
You sent me and I no longer
See you in them.

When I hear a car
Or the dog bark,
I think wishfully
That that is you,
Coming to steal
Into the house, on fire
With love and passion.

But you don't.
You have traded our love
For something or someone else;
You there in the city
Where passion may be found
On any avenue—
But not necessarily love...

When I file your poems away
I shall never read them again.
I keep them only for the promises
You made; promises you had
No intention of keeping.

When I read your poems tonight,
I was reminded of someone

Who was not what you became.
They were love letters, surely,
But you wrote yourself out of the script.
You are now in the blank space
There between the audience
And the footlights; with nary
A musician in place.

You have sought and seen my soul.
We have seen the consolidation
Of our love.  But you
Have taken the painted face off,
Wiped the grease paint away
So that I can no longer
Know you or follow you.
You have taken a backstage way out
Beyond the sets.  I stumble,
I trip across cables,
Dead-end routes
There behind the curtain.
I cannot find the houselights
Switch.  I call for you
But the silence of the darkness
Consumes my cry.
You are gone.

I shall never know who you were.
You came dramatically into my life
But exited by a backstage door.
You flourished there once,
Bowing this way and that;
Even threw kisses my way.

But I've never seen you cry.
You've always had a soft
Practised face; eyes like coal,
Eyes to get lost in.
That happened once.  We kissed
And I fell into the pools
Of your eyes, the same eyes
That now reflect my gaze:
"She loves me, She loves me not.
She loves me,
She loves me not.
She loves me not."
I can't bring flowers anymore.

# Sleeping in Sikeston

Down in Sikeston,
Where they throw the rolls at Lamberth's,
I sleep in a strange bed.
Mementos of someone else's life
Parade on the dresser, adorn the walls.

Lying there awake
Next to the busy thoroughfare,
Headlights brighten and fade
Through the windows.
I lie listening to the regular

Passing sound of tires
Against the concrete cracks
That lull one's senses to attention
For its simple regularity:
A flash and fade of light,

The *bum-bum* of two sets of wheels
And the silence that gives pause:
Sleeping under the picture window,
A prime target for a drive-by shooting;
Anticipating each car in fear,

Finding pleasure in
The mindless predictability;
That sleep will come,
And faces that peer from the dresser
Will tomorrow remain
Someone else's memories.

# The Snappers

My brother sometimes
Shoots turtles
In the family pond
With a 22,
Blowing a hole
In their god-damned heads.
My brother does this,
And has no qualms
Opening the suckers up
And poking the big soft eggs
Out with a knife.
He sometimes has to shoot
The turtles twice
Because they bite at his ankles.
My brother calls it
A son-of-a-bitch.
He does this sometimes.

# Two Virgins in a Wood

This must have been
The innocence of Eden:
He, a strapping youth
With life in tow;
She, consummate beauty
Yet to unfold.
They glance with companion kiss,
Embrace, and go.

Today, unlike the Greater Plan
Where innocence was divine,
Indiscriminate juices flow
Faster than committed spirits
May connect and grow.
Now, like wind-up toys,
They simply bump and go.

# Life in these United States

$$$$  $ $$$$  $$$
$$$$.

$$$$$$ $$ $$$
$$ $$$$  $$$$$$
$$$$$.

$$$$  $$
$$$$$$$$ $$ $$$$$$$.

## The Boy Choir

They come on a bus
From far away,
Two dozen boys—
Practised, rehearsed—
Into divination of song.
They chant, they twirl,
They trill their soprano
In madrigal,
A Mozart ensemble;
Change into sailors,
Into cowboys,
Into adults before our eyes.
They sing, they bow,
They respond like
Well-mannered munchkins
To applause.
One child smiles too much,
Too crazily.
He gets two demerits.
Marching to the bus
Single file, one boy
Chides another,
Calls him transsexual;
The boy elbows back.
They get on the bus.
They are gone;
Gone in the twinkling
Of a man's prepubertal cry.
They are us.

# Words*

*Half -utterances searching in the past,*
*grappling, groping, never last.*
*In my body, in my heart*
*and in my mind,*
*but not on my tongue!*
*And so my song remains unsung.*
                              —Keanu Reeves


*Half-utterances searching in the past*
Archives of the mind,
A mind-meld of things read or said,
The footnotes thrown out
When the last cleaning woman came in—
Whoever she was.

*Grappling, groping, never last,*
Thoughts are linear,
But words are as beads
With no thread,
Summoned like untrained bellhops,
Fumbling the packages,
The wrong floor by mistake;
The wrong bags— Peace, man!
Settle those neurons down!
Like Moses who used Aaron
As his agent,
Words may— or may not—
Come on demand.
But they always come later.
"I wish I'd said..."

*In my body, in my heart*
*And in my mind,*
These three, the embodiment
Of creativity, are patrons
In the mind-body-soul experience.
But why can't I convey
In that conversation the *depth*
With which I think
And feel and believe?
Why can I not summon
Those things as a General
With his staff?
Are all my memories,
Knowledge and vision
Mortgaged in a secret code,
Locked in that bloom upon the spine?

*But not on my tongue,*
The words do not come.
Shall the invited guests
Ignore the master's invitation,
Or have the patience as one
With a child mute and dumb,
The tongue like a rock
Lolling about the mouth?

*And so my song remains unsung,*
This life I live,
Both landlord and renter,
Bankrupt but rich.
Can you ever know the pain

When words remain unstrung,
And things are said inside
That you should hear?
If thought is linear and
*Thought* one at a time,
Shall we deliver the soliloquy
Now that you are gone
And we kick our insides
Because the orders got reversed?
And what I said in my head
Did not move my tongue in time
When you were there waiting?
The wrong words came out instead,
Like loving a song, but never
Remembering the words,
Standing there like Lot's wife,
Some sheik, immutable Rock Star?


*Thoughts on the process of dyslexia.
As surely as one may have difficulty
With *input*, so it must also be with
*output* in the thought process. The
delivery man is not *always* on time.

# Apologia

This riddle must you solve
For this quandary to resolve.
Two lads went into a wood.
And there they stood
Agape at all they heard and saw
During a winter's thaw:
The stalwart trees;
The creeks, the chickadees.

One lad was deaf and mute,
The other blind but astute.
Who of the two deserves happiness
And the rewarding bliss
Of finding his way out?
The one who points—
    Or the one who shouts?

## M.P. O'Reilly's

I waited for you at O'Reilly's,
Where the hands
Come out of the walls.
I waited through the billiards,
Watching others play.
I sat in the booth
Back in the corner,
The best-dressed guy
In the place.
I waited through dinner,
There in the walnut corner,
My face illuminated
By a 15-watt Victorian lamp.
I waited while I waited,
In from the cold there
In the Central West End.
I waited, watching people
Pass the plate-glass windows
And neon signs.
And I waited.

## Gone-away Lake

The truck labored, grinding gears
As it climbed the last knoll
That looked just nearly straight down
Into the lake, a good-sized lake—
For these parts, anyway.
A dozen cottages crowded in close
To one another, as if
Whispering among themselves
How they were to get
To the other side of the lake
Straight across—
Instead of going around.

The truck rolled down into the valley,
Laboring now to keep its speed
In check, the rear wheels squealing
Just loud enough to cue those listening
New brake shoes were in order—
If anyone cared.
The truck made the last small curve—
And the dip that came to most by surprise,
Since the old sign which read "Dip"
Had faded to that dirty, rusty tone
That old signs take on.

The driver of the very generic truck
Slowed to a stop aside one frame cottage;
He craned to view through the corner
Of the windshield.
He pulled the brake taut,

Allowing the brakes to separate;
His own hands to rest
For lack of power steering.
At the end of a long day, which this was,
The driver opened his door and slid
From his silent truck,
As shadows grew to overtake
The truck here in the valley,
Which popped and expanded as the metal
Changed its composition
Of conducting sun to that
Of the cool breeze that came across the lake;
With it, the pungent, likeable smell
Of fish, and water plants,
And other things of aquatic value.
It was a clean smell, like the smell
That makes one doubletake
At the momentary remembrance
Of a fragrance once experienced in childhood—
But not forgotten,
Locked into the power of a brain—
And a nose.

The driver of the truck
Looked to the house,
And took in at a glance
The overgrown gardens,
And the lawn that crowded
The flagstone path which led
Both to the house and the lake.
This inventory he gathered in his mind
As he walked briskly— but warily,

Down the path that split off
To the house, a 1930s house,
With a built-in porch that gave the house
A rather nervous look, as if it
Were a Pac-Man, ready to march down the lawn
Along the wood, right down into the water.
But it had been built well enough,
First as a summer weekend cottage
For city folk, who tired
Of the get-away that got-away from them
Long-distance— as far as upkeep goes.
The house sat neglected until '61 or so,
When the present owner purchased the property
And took the concerns of lawn
And peeling paint to heart.
But interest in these things die,
As many understand,
The degree of expectation
For a well-wished gift
Soon subsides into that
Of acceptance and acquiescence,
Much as it would owning a famous oil,
And remembering its worth
Only when friends come to call.

The truck driver stepped to the screen door
And pulled the door open,
Easing through onto the porch;
The door sighing quickly behind,
The closing arm using spring and hydraulic
To match again screen and screen door
That the mosquitoes attempted to navigate,

Save the whining of the dragonflies
Close at hand, maneuvering as helicopters
In formation across the front of the house,
Across the lawn and through the spreading,
Changing shadows of the hill and wood
That crept across the yard, until even
Noise and insect began to blend
Into the constant whine,
That constant wall of noise,
Unstoppable only by a falling tree,
Or unexpected footfall.

The truck driver eased along the porch
In the darkness that sifted across
The bureau, the old kitchen table,
And the ton of bric-a-brac
That cluttered the whole porch;
Like many things that graduate
Into risk and weather,
Treasured mementos of the heart
Close enough to home,
But just out of grasp
Of passing thieves.

Out of the drawing darkness
A shadow shifted,
A gentle, well-worn silhouette
Upon a sofa, from which stuffing
Poked its head out here and there,
As if in rebellion to the upholsterer
Who stapled and nailed
The material together forty years ago,

Then cursed mightily when he hit his thumb,
And banged the back of the couch
With his hammer
Until the wood was bruised underneath.

The gentle, well-worn silhouette
Adjusted itself long enough
To observe the oncoming truck driver,
Who paused briefly to greet the woman
With a peck on the cheek,
At which she turned back to look
Through the screen, to the lake,
That lapped lazily against the shoreline
Which broke the building waves
With its intermittent rocks.
The truck driver stood back long enough
To view the remnants of a TV dinner
That sat on a shelf
Next to Miracle Grow, potting soil,
And an old clay flowerpot
That brandished a decade's worth
Of little plastic sticks
That come with nursery plants
To tell you what plant it is.
The truck driver picked up
The foil tray
And carried it into the house,
Passing through another door,
Whose gentle closing was met
With a flash of electricity
As the kitchen light was activated,
Sending large slivers of light

Out onto the porch;
Suddenly cutting the thickening shadows
As with a newly-sharpened sword,
Leaving wounds of contrast
To a creeping mass.

The woman who sat on the sofa
Continued to look out toward the lake,
As if some gaze, by qualifying intent,
Could change what she saw there
Through the screen; the water
That now lapped in darkness
Below the hills that followed the lake,
Indistinctly one against
The first fade of red sky
That dimmed darker and darker
Until blackness hollowed out the heavens,
And the underside of galaxies
Sent their own black holes
And searching stars
As surveyor plummets against chaos.

The gentle and well-worn woman
Sat motionless, yet postured
As if to spring at a moment's notice.
Her hands propped her up
Like some out-of-line tripod,
Balanced only by the motor
Of a human brain there in the shadows;
Matched with reality by the sound
Of the short duration
Of a few dishes in the sink: the gurgle

And suck of the drain,
And the gentle slam of a cupboard door
And drawer.  Then silence.

The woman did not move
As darkness enveloped the house,
And night insects began
To wage their irregular orchestra
Of noise 'til it gathered about the house—
And the scream of a far-off cat
Stilled them long enough
For disconcerted attention.
Then the symphony began again.

The woman sat expectantly,
Unchanged, motionless, expressionless.
Her old features carried a determined look,
Like the time it takes
To assimilate a joke
One does not readily understand.
The truck driver emerged
From the kitchen and stood in the frame
Of the door, studying the old woman
Who sat on the old sofa,
Unwavering in her gaze through the screen
And darkness where the lake lapped
Against the shore, and a frog
Began to chant at the water's edge
Where the cattails
Resisted the small breeze
That swept over the water,
Along the yard to the house

Where the old woman sat,
Seeing, but not with her eyes.
The truck driver stepped forward
And placed a shawl
About the old woman's shoulders
Which did not move or shiver,
Nor trigger her eyes
To do anything else
But look expectantly— and vacantly—
Where no one else sees
Or could see.

The driver put his large arm
About the small woman's back
And guided her upward
And toward the kitchen door.
She walked minimally
And without destination,
As one of those battery-generated toys
That bump into chair legs, reverse,
And go in another direction
In a retinue of bewilderment.
The old woman neither resisted
Nor took initiative as the driver
Guided her to her room
Where in short measure
(But with care) put the woman to bed;
Where she lay motionless
Until he bent and kissed her cheek,
And she closed her eyes.
Her breathing did not change its pace.
It now just came softer.

The truck driver
Passed through the kitchen
And stood in the open door
That entered onto the porch.
He stood there, briefly, and swayed
To one side until his weight
And head rested against the frame.
He gave a short, quick intake of air,
And resumed a regular breathing.
He looked out through the porch,
The screen, and into the darkness.
He saw nothing.
To this he closed the door gently
And extinguished the light.
The truck driver made his way carefully—
But with skill— up the stairs
In the darkness
To where his own room waited.
The sound of footsteps on stairs
Lingered until distance
Came between the sound of them
And the hearer in the night.

The breeze that rolled
Across the water of the lake
Gave a sudden gust
Which moved the wind chimes
Just only briefly on the porch.
Their gentle cascade
Of bell-tones into silence
Was only challenged
By the fragment of newsprint

That fluttered across the porch
And alighted on the sofa
Where the old woman had sat.
Its print was barely readable.
The only thing to catch one's eye
Was the headline 30 years ago:
"Swimming accident at Gone-away,
Boy drowns, younger brother saved;
Mother comes to hysterics
Upon learning of son's fate."

And the darkness came.

N·A·T·U·R·E

*Illustrations* (left to right): a) One of nature's "Find Waldo " instances. b) A lake in Wisconsin. "Dad loved to camp and fish." c) Grandpa. "My Papa loved his fishing. His boat was always bigger than his car — and more used. I will always remember his workshop and its eternal aroma of fish." d) Geese on the Walter Steinhardt farm at Kiel, Wisconsin. e) Mary Steinhardt, mother of the author. "I weighed three pounds when I was born — and spent two months in an oxygen tent. Perhaps that explains my present aversion to camping…" f) Papa, when he was Hemingway — and before emphysema would lessen him. g) An unidentified youth at the farm at Kiel. But look at all those potatoes! As William Bendix would say, "there's *millions* of 'em!"

# First Snow

Only the first week
Of November in Missouri.
Snow fell today for our disbelief
As we watched from homes,
Shop windows; walked the streets
As it spit at our faces.

The one or two inches
Expected tonight is not expected
To stay, say passersby,
Who joke of an early Christmas
Even before the bird is carved up.
City crews are beginning
To finger Christmas decorations,
The fake garland
That sometimes catches fire
When an electrical short
Spits and sizzles
And sends a cascade
Of sparks and debris
Upon a parked car.

First snow brings these
And other things.
Though we don't get
Minnesota drifts,
We do flounder in our snow here,
Like fish do in flood
When the waters recede
And leave the ditches dry.

Man, though elemental,
Is neither ready for warm dress
Nor frost-bitten fingers so early.
The clearing of the car,
Clearing the drive,
Keeping the sidewalks dry—
These are janitorial duties on a man,
On a nation, who neither
Know nor control
The subtleties of nature,
The great first snow.

Two inches at dusk, no doubt,
Will wind up four by dawn.
The world is ice—
At least for now.
Slipping to the car,
Floundering to work,
Puzzled and anxious faces
Soon behind the wheel.
Man climatizes, accepts,
Endures the snowman's gaze
And winter's clutch.

First snows are treasured
Like most things are:
Rare, brief, expected or not;
The climax makes you shudder
Quickly back to
A metronome of reality.
The first snow brings to mind
Again just how much

We have to say about
Many things that pass our way:
Not a whole lot.
The fog or frost
That veils the glass
Keeps you watching your breath
As you peep
From your small universe
To the next,
Pausing only to wipe the glass
With the back of a hand;
Sticking the shift forward,
Getting from point A to point B.

## The Missouri River at Dusk

It's low here, now, where the sandbar
Rises and beckons your feet
That sink in sand and muck—
If you're unlucky.
The pilings that point the river center
Stand raped against the air,
Absent of the currents
That both tear and caress
And keep their anonymity.
The driftwood lies random
And exposed— much like
The hull of the Steamer Heckmann
Did in 1989 when the waters
Receded just long enough
To allow curiosity seekers
To tickle its ribs.

The water runs quick— but low—
As the sun dances on the backs
Of common fish:  the enamored
Spoonbill, the whiskered catfish,
And beleaguered gar.
They swim, knowing only
Slight depths and widths
Under a focused orange sun,
Setting the water afire momentarily
Between the bluffs and valleys
At Hermann.

From here, the 35 dead

From the Big Hatchie
Turn their skeletel remains westward
To see the mirrored vestige
Of another day dance
Reflected on beguiling eddies,
The main channel,
And a thousand ripples
In a day's life
No longer theirs or ours.

# Come, Gentle Spring

Come, gentle spring,
Wind the ivy,
Spike the iris,
Bring the trembling March.
Come, gentle spring,
Seize the fields
With greens and streams,
Flower the branches
That knock coldly
Together in winter.
Bring the geese
That forge the skies
And call for the ancient
Rites of spring
To begin again.
Great leaps and bounds
Are done in spring:
Everything brightens
To the warming sun—
Even the hell-bent
Reach heavenward,
For the supplication
Of spring.

# Ausblick

*for Jack and Ruth Haney*

The word in German
Means  "overlook."
Old hands have
Set the stones
That ring this
Curve in the road
Where tourist
And wayward traveler
Come by chance.
Here, in that fall,
Leaves, the color of sin,
Applaud the season
While we watch.
Trees, too young
To have been noticed
Fifty years ago,
Stand level against
The slope of this earth;
Where the trains
Barrel down below—
Just above the river
That goes its old way
Finding the nearest sea.
The sun draws
Long shadows here
As the tourist
Draws a long breath
Before going on—

To stand level
In this life,
Chase the train,
And choose the most pleasant
Of the many ways home.
This time at the overlook
Is all respite
In a scurrilous world
That does not see
Nor hear the walnut here
That falls and rolls
A splendid fifty feet.

## An Evening Fall

I awoke last night to hear
The burning maple leaves fall
And sweep about the house;
Having one mind to clutter
And chatter amongst themselves
A cool deception that fall has come.
I heard them say to one another
That it is a slow business
To keep the ecological hourglass
On time.  Sometimes you
Only see red.  This I heard.
The elderly lady next door
Knows which leaves fell.
I'll talk to her.

## What was That?

*for my sister Sarah,*
*who stayed overnight*
*because of the storm*

The wind at this sudden rush
Makes you bolt upright
Rightly horrified.
What was that?  The wind?
Something else?
A plane laboring overhead?
An incoming missile?
An animal in pain
Running around the shed?

No.
It seems the season
Has played a trick again.
The sound was only the wind
As it labored through the ice storm,
Moaning as it blew
Through the new icicles
Formed on the eaves
For my leery and curious view
In the morn.

# Walking the Tracks at Hermann

*for Howard Nemerov*

The silver rails shoot forward
In the direction you are going
At Hermann.  The premeditated fear
That comes with walking tracks
Is the close apprehension
Of the train behind you,
Or the ghost of a whistle
Trapped forever between the rails
That make you turn around
And check your back.

Here, where two sets of steel
Slip out of sight around the bend,
The setting sun dances on silver
And puts you at ease
Between the river and the bluffs:
Until a fast freight
Puts you to the side
Or chases you back to the safety
Of the wharf.

The distance here of mortality
Is 56 inches between two rails.
It is a good feeling, sometimes,
To put yourself at risk— especially here
Where the eaglets leap from the cliffs
In the wake of a freight;
Waver, right themselves,

And go back.
This I also do, as the sun
Goes down on an auburn river,
And the kingfisher goes home.

## The Pumpkin Stand

I remember as a boy I had
A pumpkin stand— great rows of pumpkins,
Large and small, stretching a small boy's
Mile to the road where a hand-lettered
Sign read: "Pumpkins for Sale."

I don't know if passersby
Realized the industry of a small boy's hands:
Planting the seed, watching
The springing leafy vines,
And the jubilant yellow flowers
Turned pumpkin after visitation
By the country bee.

What's remarkable in a small boy's patch,
After derelict watching
And other summer antics supplant
A boy's curiosity, is the great sudden
Reward in fall, when the once-mighty
Vines wither away and lay bare
The great orange gourds
Which solicit a quiet natural admiration
And delight over what an unattended
Garden can do.

No one stopped that fall at the farm.
I owed it to all those Bemidji city folk
Who never came my way—
Or already had pumpkins.
It was worth it just the same.

Sometimes it's just good
To put the best side forward
And let it go at that.
The seasons for pumpkins come and go,
But the memories of small boys
And pumpkin stands reign forever.

# The Quarry

By day, the quarry on Sandplant Road
Is a deep hole with giant steps
That lead down, as if some Higher Power's
Afterthought started a yet-uncompleted
Stair or some Athenian temple
Retracting into an aqua-blue pool,
Bounded on all sides by the now
Present and creeping cedars.

The quarry has changed hands again,
As if this portion of pitted earth
Can be *owned* in its desolation.
The sounds of its making sometimes echo
Within its towering walls:
The great shouts of men, the drill, the blast,
The charge of adrenalin harvesting rock.
All carry the souls of the "accidents,"
The grief, the funerals—
While business went on as usual:
Carving the land, blasting the rocks,
Shipping the blocks, until the quarry
Gave up what was to be harvested
For sake of lintel, stoop and step.
Eventually, the great hole was discontinued,
And filled with the water of two rainy seasons—
And a lake that grew as one whole pane of glass.

By being abandoned, the quarry was reclaimed
By natural virtue: the sliding rocks,
The freeze and cracks of frost—
All sent the quarry in upon itself

To become a shabby hole hidden by trees
That creep toward its edge.

While in my youth, two companions and I
Drove to the quarry, and under cover of darkness,
Ran daringly after our leader
Through a blind night,
Traversing the perimeter, clutching rocks;
Vines; sensing the edge,
Until the seemingly great distance
Was gained by perspiration, fear,
And just plain luck—
As one held back, one followed the other.

Great pains were taken to win
A youthful, silent, indiscretionary dare.
While coming around to the starting side,
The panting adrenalin of our youth
Picked up stones and threw them
Into the black blankness of the quarry pool,
Which, in its gawking mystery,
Swallowed the jeering sacrifice.
Pitted against the darkness,
The quarry pool listened, hopeful,
For the mistaken step, the cry,
The slide of rocks and debris,
And silent foreclosure of water
Over an unconscious lad, who, in his youth,
Would forfeit by step: choice, pleasure,
Opportunity— to wield or yield great fortune:
Blessedness, love, or anonymity.

God, I am sure, watches the foolhardy stunts
Of near-grown boys, who, in a void left
By a life's retinue of fallen suns,
Dance untethered, laughing at the quarry's edge,
And think in years gone past
(And this side of grace)
That the quarry is and was always only I.

# The Ringleader

Ezra Baker, the Amish man,
Passes this way sometimes.
His fringed surrey
Just touches the lowest bough
Of the grand man maple
On Maple Fair Lane.

Frost once wished
To be a swinger of birches,
Climbing a snow-white trunk
To its top to be let down again.
But I prefer maples,
Whose multi-colored leaves
From spring to fall
Shade and shower
Maple Fair Lane
When no one is looking—
And when you are.

God better provides maples
To be fierce, colorful—
And with a textured bark.
The pastels of spring
Are different from those
Of summer,
As the fiery flutter in fall
Answers and seals
Another of nature's laws:

Come winter,

Another year will have been spun
Around the inside trunk
Invisible to passersby—
Who see only
Great tiffany rolled
Beneath the wheels
Along Maple Fair Lane,
And disregard the urge to climb
For fear that winter
Will settle soon and fast
Among the loose-leaf trees
That gesture every way.

## Coming to Terms

Silence,
Howling,
Whispers,
Howling—
The next-door
Neighbor's trash
Blowing
Across the yard.
Paper plate,
Broken
Plastic forks
And spoons,
A lawn set for two.
Silence,
Howling,
Whispers.
The wind
Comes in a
Collision
Of ghosts.

# Snowspell

The snow falls in darkness
About the house.  There is no
Report on how much will fall,
Accumulate, or drift across the road.
It really doesn't matter.

Ice crystals cling to the windowpanes,
As if to see and test
The apprehension of the one within.
A steady veil of white,
Brisk, new-fallen snow
Envelopes the house, the path,
The field— even the road beyond.
Great steps are taken
To cover the tracks of man,
Who, since Boone,
Have wound a circuitous path
Through this Missouri landscape.

The snowflakes come, en masse,
To blot and cover
All that is familiar
In a February's familiarity.
Even the late-furrowed field
Slowly gives up its humps
Of upturned earth to become
One large blanket of ivory earth.

This is a mid-winter reclamation
Of a fallen world:

Great care is taken to cover
The earth with multi-formed
Six-sided frozen stars,
Whose intrinsic glory is realized
Only by the great random
And gentle anonymity—
And an appreciative eye.

This short display of white on black
Is integration of elements by force.
The elm and walnut
Of this stretch of woods
Hold forth their whitened arms
In silent boldness, plea or admiration,
For the sake of those in the wood
Who may see their heavy burden.
Even the creatures halt their activity
To crouch unseen and purvey
The great blanket from Heaven
That comes gently, then briskly,
Then gently,
Before resuming its dusky purge again.

Every aspect of the wood
Is dusted into a soothing submission.
The great silence that comes
With a gentle falling
Must come, too, with peace,
And the sobriety of the lost moment found.
Even the traffic somehow halts,
And the countryside
Turns into another landscape
Where man is alien

And Nature supreme—
Save the snow that commands respect
In the little time it is given
To cover all.

During a snowfall such as this,
The spell is Earthward from Heaven,
And nothing man can do
Can disrupt the snow
That comes without report,
Without warning from the sky,
To fall collegiately, and unbidding,
Covering the earth in white.

The first soft whispers of snow
Momentarily grate against
The old fallen leaves of another fall,
Until the whisper of frozen rain
Becomes a sullen hush—
As a verdict is read,
Preparing the wood
For the last great occupation.

The last remaining whispers
Of fallen snow come
When darkness also settles down,
And the only thing to be heard
Out of the blindness of the night
Is the crystalline spray of snow
Against the trees
Whose bark continues to be
Unyielding— and unforgiving.

But yea, the mystery of snowfall
Is just that— a continued refreshing
Dilemma.  No two flakes
Are quite the same, but come
As random crystals
In perfect fingered form,
Showing that there continues
To be a gentle order
In man's own umbilical chaos.
Snowspells take the woods:
Pure, momentary and unbidding,
As great gifts are received, sometimes—
Wordless, awkward,
But accepted nonetheless.

# Two Boys in a Field

Two boys in a field
Hold their kites aloft.
Two boys, home from school,
Guide their airy paper toys
Against and with the wind.
They check the success
Of their March wind game
With a constant discipline,
That weighs the tug and pull
Of paper on a string
Against the will of the wind,
The currents of the air.

Two boys in a field
Hold their kites aloft,
With an exhilaration
Met only by the dismay
Of one who lets
His line go slack—
And his dime-store toy
Dives to earth without ceremony,
Without joy.

Two boys in a field.
One keeps his kite aloft,
Mindful to keep a steady eye
On his kite above,
Save one moment,
In seeing loss,
Allow his own spirited
Cross of wood and paper

Plummet too, and be lost.
But it is not lost.

Two boys in a field;
One winds his string
And recovers his broken
Sullen sail.
The other watches upward,
Keeping a boy's balance
Between the rough furrowed field
And the testing tug that comes
When high above the earth
The thing of his pleasure
Raises and glories
A small boy's eternity—
Balanced against
The good and evil,
Even as among
The quickly fallen
Chinese dragons
That lie on the planet's
Windy sill.

# The Rose

First comes the stem,
The thorn,
Then the bud
Opening unto our eyes.
The color of blood
Is wrought by the thorn
And our touch,
Flowers dancing
A waltzing, top-heavy
Sway across the dusk,
The dawn;
Brilliant, majestic,
Shriveled falling petals
In a royal purge,
A dying queen's musk
Caught in a wind
Across the lawn,
Across the crowd.

As if disrobed,
The rose submits
To late summer's
And winter's claim
Of common brown and gold.
A haphazard pile of petals
Drifts awkwardly
In an autumn gust,
Irreverently,
Like royalty to the block.
Petals strewn across
This lawn and the next

Form a flower's broken, desolate,
Melancholy chain.

# Indian Spring, Indian Summer:  The Cave

*for Marshall & Eugenia Maurer*

I
*For the first time.*

What is lost here among the moss
Of Maurer's waterfall?
We stand but do not cross
The trickle that is the fall

Of water wearing into rock,
Here where the Osage sat
And left their flints from blocks,
Here upon the forest's mat.

We shall come again
When the ferns begin to wave
The way of the Indian,
Who sat here above the cave

Those many years ago.
We shall hear the rustle
And gentle pause of the doe;
The cessation of muscle

Of the bear by the creek.
Can we return to those days

Where here among the trees
A man chipped stone all day,

Here, where his soul must wind
Among these steep and stony hills
(And daily stalk his venison)
Or carrion to kill?

He must have been at peace
Here atop the hill where
Man may both lose and seek
His soul among the shadows shared

(And lengthened by generations to come—
There ought not be a place like this).


This place somehow gives hope
For the rest of the world.
For if man, in his downward slope,
Can see the past, or be re-born,

May he be redeemed in whole or part,
Here among the summer ferns?
And, if not, where may he start
His peaceful, transitional turn?

## II
*And for remembering.*

It is winter, or a long cold spring.
The wail of a child from the cave below
Makes him smile, makes him fling,
Discarded flint where others show

To have been flung by other men
Who have stopped and wintered here
And found themselves to blend,
One with nature; as deer:

Sometimes standing fast,
Thinking of the future;
Their own past,
Their own soul's suture.

## The Deep Freeze

When spring came—
As we thought it did—
We rejoiced in the southerly
Which brought forth crocus,
Dogwood and magnolia,
As though by a magician's trick.

Now, winter has come again.
The flowers and fruit trees
That raised color to the sky
Now are bent with frost
And burnished brown,
Caught stark-naked
In surprise here
Where the wind blows cold again.

But this happens sometimes
To a well-intended spring—
Or if not to ourselves.
Quick as a flower
We triumph for a spell,
And open our scented leaves
To a shower of ice and snow.

We ought not be surprised.
The children up the street
Have it that a green medusa,
Old and blind,
Lived in the willow
On the alley,
Until a northerly came

And froze her falling hair—
Perseus not far behind.

# A Wyeth Fall

*for Andrew Wyeth*

Fall has perceptibly come again.
Trees are dropping leaves:
One here, one over there,
Until the artist's palette of color
Lies swept against the fence,
The ditch, as by one
Great bristled broom.

The stubble that first was spring;
Then summer, has burnished brown
And brittle.  Grass cracks
Under querulous feet that pause,
Then go again across
The last hesitant green
That stretches spotty across the field,
Until the shadows of the wood
Cast an October spell
And swallow what has come
And gone.

The spell is broken, momentarily,
As geese, the number of fingers
On a hand, pass overhead,
The motion so close
That the sound of wings
Cutting against air may be heard:
A compression of feather
Against open sky

That keeps them aloft.
Just out of touch— they go,
Passing through man's space
Here atop the ridge,
Honking equal or greater surprise
At sharing the lengthening
Shadows of fall— ever so briefly.

The crispness of air and scene
Settles back again.
The neighbor trees
Give tremulous shudders
And cast off their burden
With frequency— or urgency.
One more Indian Summer may come—
This week or the next—
And permit a nostalgic look
At summer, until a Canadian Front
Comes to stay,
And dispels all hope for warmth.

But until then, there is now
An urgency to *see* and *know*
This parenthesis of space called fall.
The wind will blow warm,
Then cold, driving bouquets
Of summer's odds and ends
Across the road, leaves curled hard,
Mummified, scratching against
What is to come,
Preserved for what was.

Soon, the snows will come—
As they always do— and take the field,
The wood, the road;
The silence in absence of geese,
Of change, peace—
And the exhilaration before experienced
Of a memory remembered, treasured—
Of babbling brooks that race under ice
Until spring melts away the coldness,
The veiled sepulchre
Of hope already sprung.

ADAM FAMILY GREAT-GRANDPA

ROOMS
GOLDIE'S JOINT

S·P·I·R·I·T

*Illustrations* (left to right): a) The Adam family. Gustave Adam, great-great-grand-father of the author, third from left. (Adam would later become Adams. Trading a menorah for a Ford? b) A windmill on the way to California. Grandma and Grandpa would soon have a laundromat and dry-cleaning business in Pacific Beach. c) Arthur Adams, great-grandfather of the author. The Jewishness is getting watered-down… d) Papa (center) being dapper in the 1930s. e) Paul Steinhardt, great-grandfather of the author, and Papa while at Knotts Berry Farm. f) Paul Steinhardt, the business-man. He would have a hardware store and tavern/dance-halls in Johnsonville, Cascade and Plymouth, Wisconsin. Prohibition would wipe him out. (Note the advertising curtain. Great-grandpa also supplied the newest rage of the time: silent pictures!) g) Cutting wood at the farm at Kiel. Papa is at far left. Norman Glaser, Alex Stentz and Paul Steinhardt, Jr. h) Margaret Adam(s), great-grandmother of the author.

## Listen

The wind is blowing.
You know—
You've heard the sound.
It comes softly,
Building to a low roar
To ebb to silence—
A spacebar between
Two extremes.
The wind comes, goes;
Comes, goes,
One of duration:
Much like an old man
Who sends a long breath
Over a cake
With eighty candles.
The wind
Blows against the house,
The next house,
Over the town,
Down the valley,
Over the hills.
Each man, woman or child
Who listens
At this midnight hour
Holds a breath
To ponder,
That this is a simple
October wind,
Plain and mysteriously
Beautiful in all

Of its tonal scale.
It is nature,
It is the breath of God,
It is a poor man's
Pentecost.
Invisible currents
Pass over the earth,
The country, the town,
The neighborhood,
The house,
That in the silence of night
Great wreaths of wind
Are made. And I,
Singularly alone,
Find slow accord
With a westerly
That bathes all
Like-minded men.
The wind comes,
The wind goes.
It moves the curtains briefly,
Testing, soothing:
The moving force
Of fire, water,
Pitting elements against
Man who in darkness
Feels, but does not see,
The wind that comes
In October,
As a blind man's braille.

# Canto, Cantor

*for my great-great grandfather,*
*Gustave Adam*

You came into my daydreams
A Jew from Odessa.
You took the long voyage
With one of five wives—
I am told— you the faithful one—
One at a time.
You bore a portion of Israel
In your loins, your good looks,
And your charms.

I am content with you now,
You who changed your name
As a young man from Russia.
You are the secret of the family,
Dispersed here to America
Where no one would know you.
Having lived, you have died
The anonymous death,
Having traded your menorah
For a Ford, your yarmulke
For a bowler.
"There goes the Jew"
No one is heard to say.
You have traded your tribe
For the Americans;
The cultural secret agent.
I have found you out

In our genealogy;
I place crosses of stone
Upon your grave
Where you lie somewhere
Between Moses and Jesus.
Your secrecy is my unleavened bread,
My living nativity.
You are the spring
Of my wandering heart.
Because of you I do not know
Whether my search is for Odessa
Or Anastasia.

## Ode to the Good Life

Like for many people,
Death comes knocking
And takes you quickly,
Slowly; with little
Or much fanfare.
In our town
When someone dies,
Cards are put out
On the countertops
In stores to notify kin
And next-of-friends
That so-and-so
Kicked off.
That's pretty good.
Death comes on a 3x5 card
When you see it in the IGA,
And you weep your tears
In the Ravioli section
For the neighbor—
Friend or foe—
Who woke up dead.

# To Shelley—
# Who Couldn't Keep His Damned Feet
# On the Ground

To what shall we ascribe
Your short presence
And clipped genius
Among us here?
You, who rolled up
Your pants legs
To go as deep
As you could and left us
With much and little
To grasp and shake this side
Of twenty-nine years?

Shall we call out
To the waters of Spezia
And seek your soul
Waterlogged against
The bottom of your
Airy, carefree spirit?
Shall we pause
To hear the echo of your cries
Between the thunderclaps
And swells that silenced
Your keen,  provocative mind?
Shall we wish and call
Out to your atheist's heaven
To ascertain your whereabouts
In your present sphere

Of nothingness?
We think not.

The beauty you saw was tapped
From the universal good,
Which under the Creator's hand
Peeled back pages of script
In the bright rooms
That were your mind—
Which bubbled and boiled
Last on the funeral pyre,
Until Trelawny
Plucked out your heart
And set you free . . .

* * *


Verily, verily, Shelley,
You wander in Mediterranean rooms,
Cast off from your England's shore
You neglected in your flightiness;
The destiny of the greater ones,
Who, in divorcing conformity,
Mixed the souls of men
With a just man's poetry of heaven.

We shall read your words
In our leisure hour,
And let them caress our lips
As they did when uttered,
And let the poems lie,
As the occasional flower:

To bloom, be seen,
And at last admire.
Your hauntings there,
Above, upon, beneath
The fluid waters of Spezia
Will keep your spirit busy
Reconciling your great exile—
From the isle of man,
Conformity to the greater good,
Old age, and your token,
Septic funeral wine.

Grab your ashes
And mind the seas,
The money, your Timothy,
Your wife and child.
Vindicate your foolhardy, reckless self,
Before your fair hair
Finds itself upon the shore
Where pretty words
Will not suffice
To greet your lonely
Carcass there covered in lime;
Burned while Byron observed;
As your wife grappled
With her desolation;
As every man creates and fights
For victory over
His each and very own
Frankenstein.

## Pieno di Rammarichi

O, the days as a child
When I played among
The ferns and bluebells.
I was truly free.

And when I buried
My white mouse
Below the soft moss,
I placed a popsicle cross
Above his future—
And mine.

## Oil on Canvas

The footsteps come and go.
They are Oriental, they are Black.
They are White.
They are soft admiring voices,
Pausing, hard soles
On the parquet floor.
They move away.

Rembrandt, Nicholas Maes
And I are alone.
Their painted faces
Look into corners.
There are no secrets here.
The stroke of a brush
Has made the young man
Immortal, the skaters eternal—
Here among the stopwatch faces.

We are drawn into the Bruegel.
We are the travellers,
We are the hunters after heron.
We are on dirt roads
That go up and down in a life,
Frozen in memory
To be remembered later.
We are the two-faced dog.

Honthorst's woman
Holding a medallion
Is dimpled for sure.
The medallion shows a nude.
Her smile and glint of her eyes
Is an antique confession
Frozen on the main floor:
A painted face of a girl
Pointing to a painted face.
Maes' Account Keeper
Slumbers over her books,
As Cephalus, in the next frame over,
Pulls an arrow out of Procris.
All in a day's work.

## In the Company of Strangers, Loutre Island Cemetery

Here I lie
Among the cedars
Above Loutre Island,
One of many
Stretched to dust
Among the marble stones
That lean to the east.
The cold of October
Blows through
The spider's spittle
That stretches
Tenuous miles
Between harvested stones;
The spider in a balance
Between two kingdoms:
The one here,
The one yet to come.

# Imaginary Gardens with Real Toads in Them

(Upon re-reading Marianne Moore's,
   "The Steeple Jack")

I met Ambrose the other day.
He came to see me in a dream—
A dream I found composed
As I lay drifting
From consciousness to sleep
Over Marianne Moore's "The Steeple Jack."

Ambrose has gotten older
Since Marianne revised him
In sixty-one.  Since she died,
He's not a college student anymore.
And he's not confined to sit reading
"Not-native books," nor watch
Bobbing ocean-bound boats, either.
He's a priest in Kansas, now.
And he likes it.
At least that's what he was
The last time someone
Dreamed him into a garden dream.

Ambrose says this imaginary garden stuff
Is really hard on 'im.  He says
Gardens are dreams
And depending on where he's "dreamed-to,"

He usually finds his own way back.

Mostly, he's stuck as a college student—
As Marianne found him.
But he says he'd rather
Take a different occupation
Between the times people
Take him off the shelf
And read him following Marianne's line,
"Yet there is nothing that ambition
Can buy or take away."
And Ambrose says aside
He's not sure that applied to him,
Or just the line ahead.

But all the same, Ambrose is satisfied
Enough to sit and see
White boats bob along the ocean's edge,
Until someone else takes him
From the shelf and sees him
In a different garden dream.

Ambrose has a lot to say about toads.
When I saw him a second time
(He was glad I got him back)
He said he'd had enough of pastoring,
Quit the priesthood, and taken up
Gardening.  He said he'd read all
Of Crockett's books about indoor gardens

And outdoor gardens.  But he couldn't
Come to grips with the millions of toads
That inhabited the pockets
Of his camouflage vest.
He said he's not sure
What 20,000,000 springing toads
Had to do with "The Steeple Jack—"
But there they were.
He said he much preferred real gardens
And fake toads—
But that got him into trouble once.

Ambrose paused, in this mutual dream of ours,
To be sure I favored sleep
To waking and re-reading "The Steeple Jack"
And willing Ambrose back.
He paused, then went on.
He said he really appreciated
My earnest sincerity in seeing him
Through this garden dream.
And then he digressed,
Asking aside, "Did you ever wonder
What books I read in "The Steeple Jack"
That constituted "not-native" books?"
I shrugged and shook my head as if to wake
And he quickly relented, "Never mind."

The last dream I dreamed-up Ambrose,
He was clerking at the post office

Down the street from where
The steeple jack worked.  He said he quite
Liked the anonymity of this kind of job.
If he's ever needed on the other page,
It's just one jump over
And masquerading as the college student again.

He says lately he doesn't have
Too much trouble finding himself
In garden dreams anymore—
Especially with toads.
He says that's probably because
People don't dream much these days.
It had a lot to do with Miss Moore, he says,
Who doesn't pen poems anymore.
That's most of it, he says.
Although he didn't much care
For rubbing elbows with all those exotic animals
In "The Steeple Jack," they kept
The pages clean with their simplicity.

Ambrose spoke, over at the post office again,
Pointing to the steeple jack.
"Now, that's what I like about that guy,"
He said.  "He's *always* there.  That's good.
He called down to me the other day,
'Ambrose!' he said.  'From my vantage point
I've finally come to see
All that can be seen in this poem of ours.'

The steeple jack added, 'I, too, dislike it.
Reading it, however, with a perfect
Contempt for it, one discovers in it,
After all, a place for the genuine.'"

With that, C.J. Poole and the steeple jack
Resumed to gild the solid-pointed star
Atop the steeple on the church.
The steeple jack paused briefly.
Looking down, he said, "You know,
I thought I saw a woman in a tri-cornered hat.
All she did was smile— and then she was gone."
Ambrose looked up, shrugged, and was back
On the other page.
The steeple jack resumed his slow, steady work.
Ambrose was a college student again.

## Queen of Hearts

We miss you already, Diana.
You came to us in the magic hour,
A blushing bride at St. Paul's.
We were there in the carriage
With you, while you lived our dreams
Of a fairy tale come true.

You were the only one of the Royals
Who was one of us: who grasped
The hands of well-wishers,
Tousled the hair of little boys,
And accepted bouquets from little girls
Who wanted to be just like you.

You visited the homeless
And commiserated with battered women.
You were humanitarian
When it was not fashionable:
AIDs, leprosy, land mines—
Even when the Crown frowned.

Even after the kingdom fell
And they closed the gates
Of Buckingham behind you,
You stood your ground.
Where before you cried silently,
You faced things squarely.

Through shyness you gained poise.
By your human failings
You earned our respect—
And gained your crown.

You were princess of a world
So in need of one.
You were the electricity
Come into a room, a word,
A gesture— that sideways glance.
You were the mother of kings
And queen of our hearts—
A monarch who flew
Too close to the flame.

## Teutoburg Forest

O, Varus.
Had it only been a dream
That trees became men
Who followed a backslidden Roman
With wings on his head?
O, Varus.  O, Caesar.
O, Arminius.  O, Hermann.

# Attending the Memorial

*Howard Nemerov, 1920-1991*

Words cannot  express
The loss of one so loved.
But in the August requiem
Of heat, humidity,
And the one month lost,
Loss cries— or we cry—
Inwardly or visibly
For an unassuming man
In a blue-jean jacket.

For what words can express
This day that is ours
For remembering
Which is no longer yours?
You who walked Westgate
In the fall
Among the fallen leaves
And gingko trees,
And carried words in a satchel
On your back?
You who whistled
When Bach had you
Simply crossing walks
And catching sunbeams
Through leaves going home?

Where you have gone, Howard,
We do not know.

We can only venture this side
Of a mortal Jew's heaven
That as summer winds down
Your cadence of word and flesh
Stroll in the memory
Of the few, the all,
Who crossed your path
Of witty quips and wry smiles.

For this we pause in memorial
To catch a reflective glimpse,
To hear your beautiful
Deep, tonal voice again,
And seek your ghost
Among the gingko trees
That mark your runway home.

## Stars on Stars

When I think of the beauty,
I shudder.
You've seen it, too.
Away from the city
You pause in an empty field:
A sodden trekless path,
A loosely-graveled road—
And look *upward*,
Upward to the skies of night
Bedecked by jewels
Of heavenly cities.

No mirror, no atmosphere
Could reflect such beauty,
Such magnificence as a sky
So bejeweled by stars at night.
The flickering and intermittent
Twinkling of stars on stars
Humbles the most vain heart,
Comforts every choking soul;
Repairs the defective heart,
That beats by the same design
That cast a thousand comets,
Drew a celestial stair,
Or placed a twinkling light
In this galaxy— and not *there.*

Life is by design
And a basic order
That to God we would desist.
Walking in an empty field
We raise our eyes upward
To the skies and revel in their beauty;
While in our gangly ambling
We trip a heel across a web
And send a spider down
On a one and single thread.
By design, it is a world
Within a world.
The spider will remake or repair
His instinctive thread;
We, on the other hand,
Will pause, reflect,
And often as not
Reach our hands toward Heaven
And seek the God
Who is hidden there—
Hidden by the design, order,
And general placement
Of a million or so stars
Reflective of one or more suns,
That chorus both day and dark.

In all seasons
There is indeed love, hope and charity.
Short of surly clouds

To dim the view—
Or even a day's atmospheric blue—
The great panorama
Of a crystal-clear sky at night
Puts into perspective
All that can be meant by
"The hairs on your head are numbered,"
Or the ethereal
"Voice crying in the wilderness."

Man follows a certain course
In a very short generation.
May he be found worthy
(And without fail) at the end
To have come in as on a comet,
Bless his kind with kindness,
And slip away in the brilliance
Of a comet's tail.

## Playing God

I am on the telephone;
I am bored.
"Uh-huh, Uh-huh."
I fold a sheet of paper
And cut out little men.
"Uh-huh, Uh-huh..."
Snip goes the scissors:
A paper man teeters
On the edge of my desk.
Disconnected from the others,
He falls into the abyss.

# On How Things are Done in this World

When Satan smiled
To see Eve take the bait,
The sin and law
Of cause and effect
Were branded there
From Adam's "yes"
To Cain's tattoo.

Today, little has changed,
'cept for the actors
And a few studio scenes.
On a movie lot one day
A frog prince
Asked a dainty maiden
For her hand.
She said "Moi?"
He said "Oui!"
And they lived together
A cinema fable
At odds with reality.

In the real world
The face of sin
Is lit by the difference
Of "need" and "want"
Against the throes of reality.
What a toad and maiden

May perceive as going into
A sunset's eternity
May well be an Achilles' heel—
As was Japan's rising sun
And "Bonsai!" to that of
Reality and history's flashcube
Over Nagasaki that induced
An "Oh my" instead.

## Betty

When I first met you,
You were already old.
But that didn't make any difference.

I tried remembering you today.
I remember when you sat
At your desk that commanded the room,
It was as if Anastasia
Were in exile there,
Next to First Creek.
Your ever-present cigarette
Curled white wisps of smoke
Above your head,
Like oxygenated doilies.

Then you'd speak in that measured
Characteristic smoker's voice of yours,
"Ed, would you like something
To drink, a soda— a whiskey?"
I would demur to the softer kind,
And you would court your husband
With, "John, would you be so kind
As to get a drink for Ed,"
And John would make the pact
Complete, "Certainly, dear."

And then you'd bring
The reporter in you up,
"Now tell me, how are you
Doing with..." And you'd

Press for how I was doing
On whatever project I was
Working on the last time
I came over. And you didn't
Miss a beat. It was if we were
Just catching up on yesterday's
Conversation over the fence.

I would sit there in the living room
On the edge of that green braided oval rug
That stretched a whole room
While you sat there before your
Desk of papers.
There we'd swap town tales
And daily memories,
As we cast our lines of conversation,
Pulling them in gently,
Like two kids sitting on the edge of a dock,
Playing hooky.

Even when you were in a wheelchair,
And your hands were so gnarled
That there was pain in me,
You held court with the dexterity
Of a queen: articulate, intelligent,
And charismatic as always.
Our visits became fewer and far between.
But I will always remember you—
For such a friend of poets
Always casts a long sustaining shadow
Across a poet's heart. I think so.
And Dick, I know, thinks so, too.

# You, Me

You are too close to see,
Too close to write of.
Though I would attempt
To escape the chaos of this world
And write of thee and me,
I cannot, with certain inadequacy.

For you see,
We are too much alike
To know the difference
For who you are
And where I begin.

Though if I were to say
What I think of thee,
I would have to say
That you are sorrow
Wrapped in glee,
Though much better
In God-goodness
Than I will ever be.

Although my conscience
Has been pricked more than once
By thee, and your inherent
Gift of seeing behind my eyes,
I prefer the higher road

Of observation
Than walking in the shoes
Of everyone you meet.
For you see, my spirit
Is not strong enough
To endure the pain,
Walk the line,
And keep a smile straight.
I am good to rummage
Through my daily selves
And see what face will fit.

Though enamored of life,
I am not armored for life,
And my frail spirit
Does not compare to thee
Who keeps going forward
Preaching the Word:
With God in your mouth
And in your pocket.

You are one of a kind,
Taking the colossal entry
Into the city of the enemy;
Only infrequently looking aside
To the very real dangers
That Bunyan wrote of—
Much like the Trojan horse,
With so many good warriors in you.

# To Her

The nameless one I've dreamed
In the darkness of a dream.
She comes on still and windless nights,
Pale and ivory through gardens of stone;
The hedgerow— to the pool.

She comes, her beauty as music,
Her silence as strength.
There are stars in her hair
Where Orion should be.
I see her, she smiles,
She comes across the dream
To the pool where the moon
Lies double between the cups
Of lily pads. She floats there
As the moon,
Until a cloud obscures her,
She, with the starlit hair,
The ivory face, the upturned face,
Caught on a cloud back to heaven;
Celestial space.

## Dearest Phyllis

Am I so selfish as to think
I wished you'd said goodbye
Before you died?  Here, we just
Talked a couple weeks ago.

I stopped by your house today
And left a note for Frank,
"Is there anything I can do?"
I walked through the cemetery

You and I joked about,
That you had right out your door.
In a way, I was looking for you,
Walking slow, soft steps

Past the granite and marble
Neither of us knew . . .
It was seventy degrees today—
The day you died.  And in January.

When I looked through your door
To see if Frank was home,
One of your cats came instead,
Probably one of those

You liked to paint: those damned-good
Oils, the cats you said were nude.
I will always remember your sardonic wit—
And how you said you loved me—

And how I told you I didn't deserve it.
You shan't be forgotten, Phyl.
You've slipped into one of those stoic cats,
In there watching us;

Padding off to the other room.

## Wherewith He Came

Perhaps one day I shall see
The dark green slopes of Shotover:
The ramblers and tall cow-parsley
And hollyhocks that form a cover
Beyond the thatched-roof barn
That sits  beyond the Powell place;
Near the corn-ripened farms
That form a country's liesurely pace.

I may then cast my foot
Through the folded fields
That gave and then took
A life that was to give and yield
Poems from a blind man's helm,
Like so many leaves on a Milton elm.

## Omega

Sometimes my spirit says
I shan't live a year longer.
The mortal coil
That is wrapped about my soul
Cries for release.
Each muscle, each tendon—
Each step, cries for rest,
And it is not found.

I shan't know exactly
*When* my time shall come;
Whether it be the mythological
Pale rider upon a horse,
Or the passage
Into a bright expanse
Of quickening peace.
I shall not know.

But I will remember
The days of my life
Betwixt my mother's pain
Of childbirth,
And the passage of my soul
Toward Heaven.
They were, viewed at the end,
As one great wink
And one small verse

153

In this process called life.

I have no regrets:
No massage of the heart
Can bring me back.
I have entertained
A circuitous route
Of pleasure, pain
And momentary cheer.
They were days of a life
Likened to subjectivity
And a carnival run.

Truth is when you can
Shed the painted face
And be happy
In good seasons and bad.
Though the heart
May shrivel and die,
God willing,
The soul can carry
A perpetual, earnest smile...
I hope so—
At least for my soul's sake.
Now, I have
Unloaded my stone boat,
And found a small comfort
In a mortal desperate peace.

## An October Prayer

Lord, Thou hast brought autumn
To bear again
The slow turn of the earth—
So resplendent in red, gold
And yellow glow.
The light that filters
Through declining trees
Is the season's last illumination
Before the season's sepulchre
Takes the year away.

The wind now comes
More briskly from the north
And sends the stubborn flowers
And birds away.
This lack of cheer
And natural companion
Must have been
What Eden was like,
After the Fall—
An emptiness so profound
And devoid of light
As to deny that summer
Had been there at all.

When I was a child,
I dreamed a dream

In black and white of stark,
Bare branches tapping
Clear Georgian window panes
Aside a fireplace.
Tap, tap, tap-tap,
Barren branches in crisp focus—
Fruitless garden bark
Tapped against the heart.

Fall seems only for eulogies,
Dirges, gardeners
And summer's last rites.
Some people would like to fit death
Into a few days' time.
Life will gradually realign itself—
Like the newborn calf to the tit.
I feel better already.

## The Difference Between Living and Dying

The high-tension wire drawn across the soul:
Promises of heaven, prospects of below.

## Looking Edenward
(or making sense out of spiritual depravity)


Come slowly, Eden of the air.
Thy rivers run between my feet.
May I taste thy fruits
As an unabashed faithful
Shell of alabaster flesh.
May I stand resolute
Above thy rivers that flow
Out of you, growing the earth,
Keeping the good things
Going forward; never backward.
Allow us to see thy fruit
That *we* may be fruitful seeing
God's reflection upon an apple
And know His presence
Was once frozen there—
Yes—  upon an apple in God's orchard,
And not upon a pear.

# The Sea Swallow

*for Mary Steinhardt*

The tern darts,
Dives,
Plucks the fish
From
The
Water.
It hollows a nest, or,
Does without one.
Sand,
Seaweed,
Branch,
Rocky ledge.
Terns hatch
In plain surrounds.

The youth, in turn,
Traverse the length
Of the globe in a year.
Should one run
Into the hand of God,
It will plummet gracefully,
No doubt,
A descending spiral
Of feathers—
A last graceful plunge
From the first heaven.
Companion terns fly on.

My last
Remaining grandfather
Died today.
I am alone for my mother,
Who has seen the misty crag,
Experienced the high fly,
And now bears
The feathers home.
She now knows
The melancholy that comes
Only to those
In the orphanage of grown women,
Who dart gracefully
In the face
Of so much adversity;
The unbargained-for
Flight plan.

## Mowing

The boy who mows
Pits his weight and strength
Against the hill,
And the handle of the machine.
The boy presses forward,
A forelock of hair
Pointing to his work;
The machine, which revs
Unnecessarily high
(As mowers do)
Burning its mixture
Of gas and oil
That lays the grass blades down.

The mower is almost
Too much for the boy,
Who continues
An excruciating push
Of revolution
Across the carpeted earth.
He tends unknowingly
A garden of crabgrass,
Bluegrass and dandelion,
Each climbing over the other
To take claim of the yard.

The boy's sweat comes easily,

Although through this exertion
(Unbeknownst to him, perhaps)
Come lessons of discipline,
Constancy and engineering
That form the row,
The square, the final tuft
That is left behind—
And indeed makes the lawn
Look unfinished, which it is,
And always will be.

Under a young man's brow
A gospel is manifested
In the power of his gait;
His sharpened blades,
And a thousand sprigs of grass
That tip their spears
Upward toward heaven
Until they are acceptable
No longer.

# Your Mom

When you told me on the phone
That your mother died,
I was sorry to hear that.
I just didn't know.
Giving up this space
For the New Jerusalem
Is like being fitted at the store:
Looking in the three mirrors
Of the Holy Ghost,
"Is it time?  Is it time to go?"

Losing one's mother
Is losing one's first friend.
By mothers we get the genetic code,
The patient looks of an old lover
Who loved us to the end—
Two-sided playing cards:
Mother on one side, son on the other.

It is also the picking up
Of cards one at a time
In a game of memory,
Choosing shared histories;
Keeping the memory alive—
Not because of a mortal desertion,
But the planned reunion
Of a motherly resurrection.

## Prayer

Lord, how can I pray
When my heart is hard as rock?
Lord, how can I pray
When I'm mute and cannot talk?

Lord, how may I pray
So my spirit may aspire?
Lord, how may I pray
To begin and never tire?

# The Plaza After Rain

*Oil on Canvas, 1910*
    *by Paul Cornoyer*
        *At the St. Louis Art Museum*

I

Two women stand studying
Your favorite painting, Howard.
One is explaining to the other
The technique, the brushstrokes.
The women move off.

I am alone with the Cornoyer, now.
The streets glisten in their rain.
The carriages stand immobile,
Frozen in the painter's time.
One can almost smell
The dampness, the fallen
Leaves on cobblestone.
The woman with her two children
Studies us studying her.
A man with a hat behind her
Is walking away
Farther into the painting.
Is that a satchel on his back?
Is that you, Howard,
Gone into your favorite painting,
Walking the streets
Between sun and rain,

Puddle-jumping after
The museum is closed?

II
Children in the next room
Are singing a litany
Of Christmas carols.
Their chorus echoes
From room to room.
These paintings themselves
Have seen so much.
A security guard walks past
Where I am sitting,
Complaining to another:
"Where is Jerome?"
The jingling of keys
Recedes to the next room.
The guard comes back through
Again, commiserating
With the other guard,
"Is Ryce back?"
Their chatter moves on to
The next room,
Where the tree is.
The tiger-wood parquet floor
Stretches away.

It is late afternoon now.
The doors will close

And the lights will go down.
A last school tour wanders through.
"No touching," the guards repeat.
So much activity
Amid the painted snapshots.
I arise and go.
It is still overcast,
Just like in the painting.

## Snow Scene

The village contained in glass
Is lifted to eye level
And shaken like a  can.
Put down, the snow
Drifts crazily— aimlessly—
Oversized flakes of plastic snow
That swirl about
The lederhosen boy,
The daintily-dressed girl.

The family of two,
Orphans on sight,
Sled stationary in their frozen rain
That moves at someone else's will
Past the chalet, off the hill;
Where the jet stream moves
At the flick of a wrist,
A child's wonder
In the middle of July,
Practised snowfall in a pre-fab world;
A man's innate desire
To mimic God's will.

S·O·L·O

DRAWN BY EDDIE
BY HIMSELF
Nov. 25 1969
3 YRS. OLD

*Illustration:* Drawing by the author, age three. "Parents are imbued with some noble notion to save childhood mementos. Are we to see a prophecy of some promise from such things?"

## Lost and Found

At times, it is the childhood scenario:
Losing the parent in the store or mall,
The puzzlement, the quickening panic,

Each aisle a corridor of emptiness—
Or total strangers.  Running,
The child runs, runs blindly

Through a wall of tears,
The undreamed nightmare dreamed:
Abandoned, no way out

Among the grown-up racks;
The wails, the impassive looks of strangers,
Unrelenting fear.

The biological face, recognition,
Reclamation, reunion,
Lost and found,

A child's promise
Not to let go of that hand again
In strange places.

# Writer's Block

Qwertyuiop[]
asdfghjkl;'
zxcvbnm,./

'1234567890-=
~!@#$%^&*()_+
ZXCVBNM<>?

## Night Demons
(a discourse on insomnia)

Here I am, an accursed insomniac at 34.
I head for bed, get a sudden surge of energy;
Do some paperwork,
Scan the TV channels,
Surfing among the national anthems
Signing off, stiffening at the thought
Of the forthcoming static.
When will it end?  When will the sleep
Of my childhood return?
Even if only half-energized?

Here I am again,
Wandering my rooms,
Sitting at the piano at two in the morning,
Finding a melody; maybe not.
Can't play too loud—
The neighbors might hear.
Back to bed, reading a mystery,
Seeing its resolution to the end;
Disappointed I had to put it down.
Off to nibble: a peanut-butter sandwich.
Television again, a video,
An action flick I've already seen
A half-dozen times.
I am comforted in the chemistry
Between Keanu and Sandra—
Even Dennis Hopper's madness.

And I think of my own gentle madness—

The mysterious and arduous dreams
That tire me more than day-work:
Speeding, sliding off the road like last night;
Being hunted by bad men,
Averting danger, winning
What I can remember;
Tangible relatives— my younger brother
And sister frozen at a younger age;
Our living together with Mom and Dad;
Even Wally, the brother I somehow
Didn't like but can't pinpoint why.
I tumble, I hide in rafters,
I am being sought out,
I am on the side of right,
A tableau of good and bad.

These dreams are extensions of the day—
But more rigorous.
I dream-sleep so deep
I sleep through the *beep-beep*
Of the alarm I hear but cannot arise to.
I am caught in the flickering signals
Of REM; the room has turned cold,
I cannot get up. I somehow manage to
Pull the woolen blanket over my head
To re-breathe the warmth of my own air.
I'm held hostage by dreams,
So close to the edge of consciousness
That I must be reminded of the difference
By my surroundings on waking.
Do I fear to sleep? Are there mental demons
Waiting for me, or am I being saved

Through my evening's working-out?
Is this my self-inflicted therapy,
An exile into short jumping stories,
That rival or better real life?
Is this my unconscionable hell,
Fallen there by decreased pulse
And respiration?  Should I die in this
Exile from day, shall I be able
To import the great white light
And heavenward comforts adequately,
Or be doomed to this purgatory
That goes on non-stop, switching
Plots and frequencies enough
For me to fall back into
Its dreamscape unbidden?

But having surfaced rested,
Would I have remembered all that came
Seemingly moments before;
Some great thespian outrage
Or Academy Award-winning scene,
Some dream-motif set up
By a day's doings, as unconscious
And subliminal as reminding yourself
To breathe.  Having fallen asleep quickly,
Might I have laid-away my orders
For the do's and don'ts, pre-set, perhaps,
By the last conscious passage
Of a mystery book, a biography,
A day's frustration?  May the remedy
Be found asleep, a symbiotic
Push and pull of pulse and breath;

Surging blood, cells darting to and fro
In a genetic wake— a wake of ebb and tide—
And that of an inner fretful, watchful
Waiting.

How many more times shall I enter
The dreamscapes again,
When I am the narrator in the dream,
The good guy, the one running
From fears manifested in the form
Of a "bad guy," seeing those familiar
And familial, having no choice
Of word or deed with those
I would not consciously welcome,
Put there as chess pieces in a
Black and white melodrama
(I can't remember dreaming in color)
'Til I comatose-awake more tired
Than when I surrendered...

Answers: I see none.  Relevance: none.
I am a worshipped detective serial
In my own individualized tailored
Sleep-wave, caught in a tide
Of kinetic energy, until my battery stores
Have released their power, amperage
Sucked dry by a dehydrated rinse cycle;
Accosted by a director's cuts,
Film-flicks cast by someone else,
A CSA derivative of the Invisible Man,
There, gone, no one fully in charge;

Only serialing non-stop,
Waiting for me to fall into it again
Without preparation, prescription,
An owner's manual,
Or a ticket out.

## 12:37 A.M.

I walk this night
Up along Bayer Road,
A singular tar and chat lane
That goes along
The upper edge of town.
Here, where my feet
Register footfalls,
My eyes half-close
To contain the thought—
That exercise and peace
May be found in this
Evening walk.

As I pass the Eikermann's,
I consider other lives,
Other forms bent to sleep;
Late-night television
And other diversions.
Since no lights flare
From this house,
I think how
Nathan and Nicole
Must be sleeping
Their pre-teen dreams
Of Little League games,
The high pop fly;
The two runs home—

While I walk this road
Planning grown-up strategy
Against the darkness,
The sodium lamps,
And the bugs that dance
Across the moon
With its borrowed light.

# Half and Half

*for Lynn and Rhonda,
    at the Rock House Cafe*

When I am sick
And bereft of sleep
I remember how
The children of Israel,
After Moses struck the rock,
Wept for Egypt
And the Pyramid Bar & Grill.

When I get ill
(And I get sick quicker)
I moan and groan
How *tomorrow*
I'll change the diet;
That in surviving
Another spell,
I offer promises
Of giving more time
To myself (and quiet).

Then I dream nightmares
Of giving up Hostess
For vegies, and handing out
Celery sticks
To everyone I meet, with a
"Good Day," and "God Bless,"
While children I do not have
Pick walnuts

From my neighbor's tree,
And secret them away
Within our house
For, as they say,
"So our family
May always be,"
Exegete cousins
To the common mouse.

I would be happy
With mama,
And my food
Stir-fried, baked,
Crisped, even chopped.
But don't take away
My junk food
(less one banana);
*My* cholesterol,
*My* triglycerides,
*My* stopped-up heart,
And my beef people's
Picture of the fatted calf,
Sacrificed
In this Gentile's kitchen
Of fat, Ovaltine,
And a generous portion
Of Half and Half.

# Dandelion Dreams

I

I wonder, as I lie in bed
One hour past midnight,
How many others share
My very same space of insomnia.
I wonder who lies, hearing
The same evening ghosts of wind
That wail through the open storms
During this dandelion spring.
I wonder who lies
Beseeching the wind's translations,
Coming to its momentary crisis,
As two lovers who slow to moan.

But this is not love— it is mystery.
The insomniac watching *Night Heat*
In a closed room will not
This evening know
The open message of the wind
As sung through a harmonica of walls.
It is I, and I alone,
Who will hear the shade
Scratch the window as it does,
The bark of a far-off dog
With its own attention
Upon something ordinary

This side of day.

II

It is all relative.
The wind that now sends
A gentle current
Through the house this night,
Comes so as an unexpected,
Appreciated guest.
The wind that softly whistles
Also comforts the children
In the Projects
Who sleep with the wind's
Silent feathery touch
Across their backs—
Just as their pappies years ago
Stumbled through the Projects
That were only then
Fields of dandelion dreams.

## Tracking, or Exploring the Psyche in November

Here I am, survived another day.
The house greets me
As aloneness knows the kinship
Between two brothers who do not talk.
Darkness of the evening house
Is met by the inviting evening lamp,
As the rays of day are met
By sunlit rays through blinds
In a coarser way.
The aloneness— light or black—
Are two extremes,
As were the dark of womb,
And in a few score years—
The migrating tunnel
Of lightened death.

Oh me, taking to write
Drearily again: of empty houses,
Empty chairs, unvisited stairs.
A great company of ghosts walks here:
Those that I have imagined,
And those that come and go
Without your asking—
From one house to the next.
For, you see, we are all
In the company of ourselves,

Given to entertain or nullify
The driest hour; illumine
The most-quiet night.
We are what we make ourselves,
What we perceive the mirror to be—
Our soul to go where it may.
Slipping out of doors,
We come home to ourselves—
The ones we have fashioned
From the shelves in our mind:
The good word, the ill; the good deed,
The chill, and the number of others
We occupy within ourselves.
It is frequently good
To keep some doors closed,
Both out of sight—
And those of the ghostways.
Great trepidation and consequence
Come to those who seek their psyche—
Contract therapy, or the written word.
Allow what is going on
To keep going on in the mind;
Only peek occasionally
Past the upstairs doors.
The Subconscious and Will
Will find their bumbling ways
Much easier than with the help
Of one or two amateur Clouseaus—
And certainly Freud.

After all, wasn't Freud
Just a dirty old man?

## Shutter Speed

Where do we go when we sleep?
Do we go to other lands
Through darkness into light,
Weaving down passages
To the edge of our souls?
Do we climb ladders back
To enter the next room
Of the dream, carrying
Only enough wax and wick
To see our way through?

Do we hail a dream-boat,
Booking passage across
The next rising tide?
Are we our daily magicians,
Spinning ourselves a spell
To come back unharmed?
Do we go to an isle
Where all the dreams
That have been dreamed
Are kept, and pick
One of our choosing;
To take a dream from there—
Stacked like cordwood—
To leave one in return?

And having gone and returned

And found ourselves
Not in need of rescue,
Do we journey out again
Down the avenues
Where moons and planets
Spin on either side,
From our universe to the next?
And having done our shopping
Of this plot or that—
And who may be cast
In this play of ours—
Do we leave the program
On the floor
And rip the ticket up;
Having returned
Only after going,
By way of another electrical
Cerebral admission?

# Thoughts on Turning Thirty

It's depressing as hell,
Actually.
Though at this point
I'm faring better
Than Keats at his age.

Friends joke, cajole:
"The Big 3-0, eh?"
And I wince and wish
The transporter
Wasn't fiction on *Star Trek.*

In all of this,
I still continue
A three-score desire
For steady employment,
A shampoo to cure
Male-patterned baldness,
An average girl
With medium breasts—
And a dog named Elvis.

# The Shadowlands

We are shadows thrown upon the wall.
We are images, what others see;
How we see ourselves, true—
Or what we think we perceive
Or want to be.
We are shadows, souls in circumspect,
Flesh and blood souls
Who love, hate; lie and get up,
Fall and desist.
Our emotions are our ramparts,
Our will: our army;
We of our several selves
Count in unison and apart.
We go forward alone and together,
Seeking the childhood of our nursery,
While gaining the world
By grown-up design.
We are scared of living, yet wither
At the thought of mortality.
We think that in loving
Aloneness may be less lonely,
But it is not.
We pass one another on tracks
Of a variable gauge,
Locomotives bound
For this dream or that;
Our own stationmasters
With our own rules,
Solitaire by cheating;
Playing with more cards, or less—

We are the poker-faced children
Who lie but do not deceive,
Caught red-handed in the secret garden,
Having purposely lost the key
So as not to be incriminated.
We choose to remember backward;
Not forward— taking less the prize
But the reception crumbs instead.
We are the invited guests
In a stranger's house,
Being by being, but somewhere else.
We look to the window
While talking; hearing— but not.
We seek the lands and fair weather
On the other side of the glass,
A mind-manufactured substitute
For the present tense.
We look into the fire
And see what is not there,
Secret arsonists who see something
The firemen do not.
We shake with the fever of a spell,
A magic of incredulity
And unbelievability,
A terrestrial credo of faith
Against hopelessness and helplessness.
For in believing in our separate selves
We hold ourselves to treason,
Taking life on as in a trinity;
Going forward with condemnation
And absolution.  We change our souls
Even as we spring forward and fall back;

Toddlers who waver but do not yet run,
Children who parry, but mind the switch,
Adolescents who grow up
But have not the answers.
We take the first bicycle ride,
And absorb the first panic;
Then free-wheel through the wind,
Seeing the twilight shadows
That gather and stretch across the road,
An intermittent projection
Of brilliance-darkness, brilliance-darkness.
We rocket with temporary momentum,
Believing while feeling, feeling to believe,
That one's shadow melds with the others,
And becomes darkness
So that there may be light.
We go forward many times into darkness.
We fumble, we waver, we go into a ditch.
We remember the majesty of the thrill
Made moreso by the fall.
We pick up our bikes as children,
Go forward as through many lands,
Tourists by design— or bad directions.
We visit this place and that place
Within ourselves,
Opening shutters here and there
To both feel the rain of the storm—
And shut it out.
We exult, we distress,
We shuffle the cards,
Deal them out.
We gather storms

To make our own rain,
We press our nose
To the glass of our soul
And think that whatever should come,
Tempest or not,
We will see our own
Shadow cast upon the wall.
We will remember that
We are our company in our aloneness,
That our image is that
Of belief battling unbelief,
Both in ourselves
And when we are in the shadowlands.

## Remembering the Dreams

You reach your pallet
Every night at the accustomed time
And surrender your length
In a room set aside
For your unconscious wanderings.

The mortal coil curls, stretches,
Turns upon the bed.
Consciousness gives way
To unconsciousness
And the dreams that come
Cajole, comfort, put you at rest
Between the flickering images
Of lust, horror, and terror of dreams
That scream unbidden
Across the mind's mental screen
Of flickering shapes,
Faces, and forgotten things.

The sun caresses you from sleep
Dipping across the yard,
Into the yard,
Until the great flash
Beckons your body up
Through slit eyes
For another day:
A retinue of slow starts,

Low pay, slow hours,
That raise the memory
Of your dreams
Just long enough to say,
"That was a shitty dream,"
And forget the dreams
That came and went
Between the western
And eastern suns.

**E**DWARD J. STEINHARDT is a poet and writer who resides in Hermann and University City, Missouri. He is a member of the Poetry Society of America and the Academy of American Poets. He is also a member of the Missouri Writers' Guild, serving as that organization's president from 1994-1995.

*Dandelion Dreams and Other Poems* is Mr. Steinhardt's second book of verse. His previous book, *The Painting Birds,* was released by the Westphalia Press in 1988.

Mr. Steinhardt is also editor of *Voices: Poems from the Missouri Heartland,* released by Dormer Window Books in 1994.

Mr. Steinhardt is founder and coordinator of the Missouri Writers Week Award for Poetry, a program which annually recognizes verse written by Missourians.

For several years he sponsored the inaugural ceremonies for Missouri Writers Week, which featured U.S Poets Laureate Howard Nemerov, Richard Wilbur, Mona Van Duyn and poet Charles Guenther.

The most recent ceremony, in honor of the Missouri Writers' Guild's 80th anniversary, was held in the Rotunda of the Missouri State Capitol.

Steinhardt also is a journalist. Those efforts have earned him several awards, including Best Historical Article, Best Regularly-Published Newspaper Column and Best Newspaper Article in Missouri.

**C**HARLES GUENTHER, author of the introduction to this book, is one of the world's most acclaimed translators of poetry.

In 1973 Mr. Guenther received Italy's highest decoration, the Order of Merit of the Italian Republic, in the rank of commander, for his many translations of Italian poetry.

He is also the recipient of the James Joyce Award from the Poetry Society of America, the Missouri Library Association Literary Award, the French American Bicentennial Medal, and both the Webster Review translation prize and Witter Bynner Poetry translation grant.

Mr. Guenther has published in more than 300 U.S. and foreign magazines and anthologies. He is the author of eight books of poetry and translations, including *Modern Italian Poets, Paul Valéry in English, Voices in the Dark, The Hippopotamus: Selected Translations* and *Moving the Seasons: Selected Poems of Charles Guenther.*

Guenther's book, *Phrase/Paraphrase,* earned him a nomination for the 1971 Pulitzer Prize in poetry.

Mr. Guenther lives in St. Louis, Missouri.

# *Index by Title and First Lines*

**DANDELION DREAMS AND OTHER POEMS**
was composed in Palatino